PERCY ROWE was born in England, served with the Royal Air Force as a navigator in World War II, and came to Canada in 1946.

Since that time he has been a newspaperman, first with the *Winnipeg Tribune* and then the Toronto *Telegram*. He has been reporter, foreign editor, literary editor, and assistant news editor, and is now assistant managing editor and travel editor of the *Telegram*.

His travels have taken him all over Europe, into the U.S.S.R., to parts of Africa, Asia and Australasia, across Canada several times, through much of the United States, and to most islands of the Caribbean. Many of these journeys have included visits to vineyards and wine cellars of note—and wherever he goes samples the native vintages. Although he does not consider himself a wine authority (he debunks that term in this book) he is a wine lover.

He is married and has five children, three of whom are now old enough to join him in enjoying a good glass of wine.

Jordan Wine Company   Chalet Wines
Barnes Winery
Brights
Chateau Gai Wineries
Parkdale Wines (Normandie Wines)
Turner Wine Company
London Winery
Beau Chatel Winery
Andres Wines
Abbey Wines   Modern Wineries
Calona Wines   mentioned
Growers Wines Company
Villa Wines
Casobello
Mission Hill

The
WINES
of
CANADA

The
WINES
of
CANADA

Percy Rowe

MCGRAW-HILL COMPANY OF CANADA LIMITED
TORONTO, MONTREAL, NEW YORK, LONDON
SYDNEY, JOHANNESBURG
MEXICO, PANAMA
DUSSELDORF

THE WINES OF CANADA

ISBN 0-07-092781-2 / FIRST IMPRESSION, 1970

PRINTED AND BOUND IN CANADA

Contents

Foreword

THIS book, the first of its kind on the specific
subject of Canadian wines, has been written with
the help of many people – winery company executives, winemakers, scientists, grape growers, and
government officials who work in the offices, wine
cellars, laboratories and vineyards of Canada.

One man especially must be singled out from the
anonymous many. John K. Couillard, general manager of the Canadian Wine Institute, has over a
period of more than two years been my travelling
companion, introducer to the knowledgeable, men-
tor, adviser, and – at the proof stage – corrector of
errors. Without him, these chapters could never
have been written. Although Jack's title might appear to give a certain official cachet to the work, I
should like to point out that all the opinions ex-
pressed herein and any inaccuracies which may have
escaped his perception are wholly mine.

CHAPTER ONE

The Magic Of Wine

WINE, any wine, and certainly Canadian wine, is cellared in mystery – like the birth of children, or royalty, or genius.

Like most aphorisms, this is a paradox. Thousands of words have been written by poets and scientists about wine (although not about Canadian wine). After-dinner speakers and chemists have tried ever harder in their praise or explanation of the fermented grape. Yet we don't know everything about it. The day will be a sad one if we ever do, for then it will become like everything else we eat and drink. At present – and, thank Bacchus – for the foreseeable future, it is entirely unlike any of them.

You don't believe this sweeping statement? Then when did you last sit down and, in detail, discuss a steak, or even a lobster?

Perhaps, though, we should keep to liquids. How many adjectives are there to describe whisky? The ad men have come up with mellow and aged, but when did you hear anyone, rattling his ice-cubes, use them?

Beer? There is only one that you will hear and that's "flat." "Flat" beer is so rare nowadays that the product is virtually languageless.

Soft drinks? They may be zippy, zingy or tangy — their drinkers never say so.

But wine has a never-ending vocabulary. It is as if its lovers were straining for new ways of description as lovers are wont to do. It is not simply "good." To use a miniscule sampling of the thousands of adjectives that have been used, it may be dry, earthy, fruity, sweet, cloudy. Or if you prefer a wider choice, there are petillant, sparkling, new, young, middle-aged, old, dead, purple, deep red, brown, tawny, straw-colored, golden, greenish, rosé, onion skin-colored, neutral, sharp, yeasty, sour, corky, foxy (a description specifically reserved for Canadian wines and derived from the Fox grape), acidy, flinty, vinegary, sulphurous, fragrant, Madierized, soft, hard, rough, full-bodied, puckery, flat, clean, metallic, tart, bitter, well-balanced, well-bred, with "character," distinctive, elegant, luscious.

Or how about lusty, robust, hardy, heady, gay, shy, austere, pretentious? Or perhaps mischievous, muscular, neurotic, companionable, lively, serious, authoritative, spirited, generous?

Enough? Possibly, but one could go on and on for there are certainly more ways to describe wine than the 600 synonyms that exist for drunkeness in the Finnish language, even more than the reputed 1,400 ways of saying "bombed" or "stoned" in the English language. These are unfortunate descriptives because wine, for the most part, is the drink of moderation. This may be because wine drinkers are so busy thinking up new adjectives, they don't drink too much.

Katharine Whitehorn, the English writer, has tried to save time. In her usual amusing way, she has told how she writes S to represent all wines she encounters at tastings which are soft, mild or bland, and IF for those which are sharp. The S and IF stand for soap and iron filings.

Most wine drinkers, even the most humble, are not content with abbreviations, possibly because they are more liberal in their praise. Consequently, since the still unprecise date when man first tasted fermented grape juice, a vast compendium of eulogy has built up.

There are hieroglyphic bouquets for wine from Babylon and Egypt; there are 165 references to it in the Bible, where Noah — ten generations after Adam — is mentioned as the first to plant a vineyard; and Homer in 850 BC could say, "wine gives strength to weary men."

Indeed, it seems at times that philosophers have had their heads turned to poetry, and poets have un-metred their verses so they might better philosophize on the subject of wine.

So Plato could say, "Nothing more excellent or valuable than wine was ever granted by the gods to man".

And Omar Khayyam came right back with,

> I often wonder what the vintners buy
> One half so precious as the goods they sell.

Rabelais, Goethe, Milton, John Gay, Thackeray, Clifton Fadiman, hundreds more, have joined the race with their testimonials. Not only professional writers praised wine. Its allure has had words slipping from pleasured tongues in songs, sayings, and lengthy anecdotes, for centuries.

To take one lone sample, who was the unknown to first utter the French adage, "dinner without wine is like a day without sunshine"?

Some have even married themselves to wine. George Saintsbury is still the most notable example. *Notes of a Cellar Book*, first published in 1920, covers 31 years of his collection and drinking of wines. He started with a few dozen bottles of wine and recorded his experiences in an ordinary exercise book "cloth-backed, with mottled paper sideboards outside, and unruled leaves within." Saintsbury was able to say, "There is no money among that which I have spent since I began to earn my living, or the expenditure of which I am less ashamed, or which gave me better value in return, than the price of the liquids chronicled in this booklet. When they were good, they pleased my senses, cheered my spirits, improved my moral and intellectual powers, beside enabling me to confer the same benefits on other people. And whether they were bad or good, the grapes that yielded them were fruits of the Tree of Knowledge which, as theologians too commonly forget to expound, it became not merely lawful but incumbent on us to use with discernment."

Drys, please take note, and remember that this came from a man who for some years could write lovingly about claret and burgundy, although for health reasons he was not allowed to drink them. Saintsbury, by the way, suggested that wines might be named after women or songs. A more recent author rather unromantically but no doubt overpowered by the influence of Detroit, has likened various wines to different models of cars with humorous sketches to match.

It was Saintsbury who used one of the most unusual descriptions for a wine: "mauliest." This brings us back to that partial list of adjectives mentioned earlier. You will note that many were not complimentary. This is because wine lovers are not blind drinkers. Only the other kind of love is proverbially myopic. No, wine drinkers look, smell, taste and savor; above all, they judge. There is no other food or drink about which people are so critical.

If the customer who is the drinker trusts his senses so implicitly, it behooves the winemaker to do the same, so, in the last analysis, all those associated with the Canadian wine industry rely on the look, smell and taste of wine just as the winemakers of Europe, South Africa, Chile and California have through the centuries.

There could be – God forbid – a chemical analysis printed on each bottle in the way of some flossy delicacies, but wine defies chemistry. The same percentages could appear on the labels of two bottles, yet the contents of each would taste different to the same bibber.

It is true that every winery in Canada has its own lab full of white-coated gentlemen, formulae, yeasts in refrigerators and bottles of wine being tested, but each winery also has a room, generally pleasant, with leather chairs, timbered walls and an air of relaxation, where the ultimate examination goes on – the final test of colour, smell and taste.

And not only there is testing done. Horticultural experimental stations and liquor board headquarters across the country have their laboratories, but won't deny the importance of the physical qualities.

And not only there either. For 25 years, once monthly, except when the harvesting and crushing of grapes kept everyone busy, representatives of winemaking companies in competition, liquor boards, and the agricultural sciences have met for an afternoon in the private room of a hotel off the Queen Elizabeth Highway between Hamilton and Niagara Falls to test wines for colour, smell and taste.

I should use such fancy terms as bouquet, body and robe, but having participated in one of these rituals, I cannot bring myself to do so, for wine tastings of this nature are first and foremost, workmanlike events. There are no pretty labels on the bottles because these are "blind" tastings. There is no candlelight, but simply a long table covered with a white tablecloth. There is no soft music for there can be no distraction. The only view is of Lake Ontario. On the table before each of the 20 or so tasters are five glasses at a time, a scorepad, a dish of small pieces of cheese to clean the palate, and a cardboard spittoon.

The work begins. An official of the Canadian Wine Institute, which represents nearly all the winemaking companies in Canada, pours a dribble of, for example, a medium dry white wine into one of the glasses before each taster. He repeats the process with four other bottles. The tasters lift the first glass – No. 1 on their scorecards – and raise it toward the light. They grade from 0 to 10 for clarity, the same for colour. Then they put their noses deep into the glasses and sniff. They grade 0 to 30 for bouquet. Finally, they take a sip, swill it in their mouths, spit all of the sample into the spittoon, grade 0 to 50 for flavour, occasionally put a few remarks in the column provided, nibble a piece of cheese, and then begin again with No. 2.

Apart from the tiny clink of glasses, the gargling of the wine, the expectorations, there is silence. No one talks. This is much too serious a business. This isn't the type of wine-tasting party which has become so popular a part of Canadian home life, where guests drink the samples. In fact, it's a frustrating experience for the stranger. I sampled 20 wines and spat them all out when I was there before I was allowed to drink a glass of wine at leisure.

It would, of course, be the ideal spot to take the wine snob, who thinks the only wine in the world comes from a certain half acre on a certain hillside in France (but has never actually drunk it) and turns up his nose at all Canadian wine, as well as Australian, South African, Californian, and Portuguese.

It would surprise him to learn that imported wines are also tested. These "sleepers" appear unlabeled with the Canadian products and don't rate any higher than some wines bottled in St. Catharines.

"Ahhh," says the snob, but of course what can one expect? The tasters are Canadian, true, but members of the Canadian wine industry have come to this country from all parts of Europe, return there frequently, and know European wines. Additionally, there have even been guest tasters from Europe. Canadian tasters merely consider themselves members of a quality standards committee meeting, the official name for these sessions. But they all, through their work and for pleasure, have tasted a great variety of wines. When they roll a glass in their warm hands to bring out the bouquet of a red wine, or write in the remarks column, "raisiny," "tastes of the vats," "it's like friar's balsam," "a poor wine – it has been left in the tank too long without sufficient sulphur dioxide," they do so with experience.

Canadian winemaking is based on the age-old ways of making wines, but with all the advantages of modern science and hygiene. There are no vintages, but instead wines are blended to achieve a top-quality product regardless of year.

Above all else, Canadian wines differ from other wines of the world because until recently they have been made essentially from the once-wild native labrusca vine which is as distinctive as the McIntosh apple, another all-Canadian product.

Grape wine is both a simple and yet tremendously complicated product; perhaps it was first tasted by man accidentally. Grapes may have been left to ferment, thus making a simple wine. If the vines were cultivated, it must have meant that the first wine drinker was no longer a nomad, as it takes some years for the grape vine to bear fruit. In any case, if our first wine drinker liked the taste, it is almost certain he told his neighbours and they all settled down, preferring the vineyard to the forest.

Nobody is sure who those first wine drinkers were; some have suggested they were Chinese. If that is so, it was a long time ago because Babylonian tablets and Egyptian carvings depict the manufacture of wine more than 4,000 years before Christ. Archeologists tell us that in more recent times there was a winery at Gibeon, near Jerusalem, which was built in 2,600 B.C. It had storage for 30,000 gallons. The Phoenicians subsequently brought wine to

Greece, the Greeks and Romans developed viticulture and the Romans took it into western Europe. By the 15th century, winemaking was part of the way of life in France, Germany, Italy, Spain and Portugal. The English couldn't be bothered. They had other means. In 1152, Henry II of England married Eleanor of Aquitaine, thus commencing 300 years of English rule of the best wine areas of France. By the middle of the 15th century, three million gallons of wine were leaving Bordeaux yearly for England.

Not only the English and French fought over the vineyards, however. Men through the ages have possibly treasured them more than their wives. Thus, today we find that in Tuscany the most esteemed vineyards for the making of Chianti have been in the same family for 900 years – and that the largest vineyard owners in Ontario took little time to reject a subdivider's price by realizing that without their vines, with nothing to do and so much money, they would, after the inevitable world trip, run the danger of sitting down and becoming alcoholics.

Wine, which may have been the nectar of legend and certainly has been treated as such through the centuries, is a natural product. The grape is the only fruit that will preserve itself because it contains fermentable sugars and because on its skin there are natural yeasts that change the sugar into alcohol. This is the basis of all winemaking. It isn't as simple as all that, of course. The grape also contains B vitamins, traces of 15 to 20 minerals, more than 20 organic acids. About 625 of these grapes are needed to make a bottle of wine. If allowed to ferment under the wrong conditions, they will make not wine, but vinegar. And if not straight vinegar, something that is as likely to be as unpalatable. So, in modern times, winemaking has been controlled, largely by the forces of science.

One example: The skin of a single grape can carry up to 10 million yeast cells, of which a one-hundredth are wine yeast cells. 100,000 cells are very difficult to regulate. One or a hundred may go marching off in the wrong direction, and ultimately produce the wrong kind of taste. So all the natural yeast cells are destroyed by Canadian winemakers and replaced by cultured yeast cells because it is known almost precisely how the enzymes of these cells work in fermentation, what they are capable of, what tastes and smells they produce in the resultant wine.

Perhaps this all sounds a little too unmagical. We had better return to the simple elements of the vineyard. Essentially, there are only three factors, the vine, soil and the weather which control the type and quality of wine.

Andre Simon, one of the world's great authorities on wine, has written, "Judging from the wines which I had the privilege to taste in many parts of the world, I am of the opinion that fine wines can be made almost everywhere where the vine will grow and grapes will ripen".

These grape growing and ripening areas are almost wholly within the 50th and 40th degrees of latitude in the northern and southern hemispheres which, incidentally, have been historically the regions of man's greatest civilizations. Canada's two vine growing areas, the Niagara Peninsula and the Okanagan Valley of British Columbia are squarely placed within these geographical boundaries. However, it is possible that future changes in ecological and climatic patterns may extend the world's vine growing areas.

In the Niagara Peninsula, which grows at least 80 per cent of the grapes now used in Canadian wines, older grape growers frequently refer to the warmer winters of the past 25 years compared with those which killed off vines in the early part of the century. Homes, factories, the exhaust fumes from automobiles on the highways have all brought a warming influence. Previously, there were only two reasons for this peninsula being the main grape growing area of Canada: the moderating influence of Lake Ontario on one side, and the long low range of hills protecting it from the north winds on the other. Now one-third of all the grapes grown there are picked from "up the escarpment," which usually means over the escarpment. First one grower, then a dozen, and now scores found they could grow suitable wine grapes without protection from the wind.

Niagara and British Columbia could hardly be two more dissimilar areas to accent how widely grapes will successfully grow. The peninsula in Ontario is generally flat with a moderate rainfall; the Okanagan Valley is, where undeveloped, a sage-brush desert surrounded by mountains. Nearly every vineyard slopes; each has to be irrigated. Sunshine is abundant in both areas, although it is generally far hotter (not infrequently topping 100 degrees) and far colder during winter in the Okanagan. Both have more sun than many of the world's renowned vineyards — for instance, in Germany or northern France.

But climate is only one of the three ingredients in the recipe. Soil is another. To anyone who has seen the shale-covered near-cliffs on which the vines of the Moselle grow or the waterless plain of La Mancha where the grapes for many Spanish wines struggle, there can be only one conclusion: the Canadian grape grower is very fortunate. It may be that vines, like roses, don't require the best of soils, but it is better to start with earth rich in constituents, particularly when the roots of grape vines may stay in the same spot for 100 years.

These vines are the last key piece in the jig-saw of winemaking, but there are nearly as many kinds as there are people. The preponderant species in Europe and Africa, vitis vinifera, has 5,000 known varieties. Other species have 2,000 varieties. In Canada, the species originally and still preponderantly grown is vitis labrusca. In addition, grape breeders like those at the Ontario Horticultural Experimental Station at Vineland and some wineries are developing new hybrids, as are grape breeders throughout the world. This means today that Canadian wine is made from grapes called Concord, Delaware, Bath, Agawam, Marshal Foch, Himrod, President, Iona, Niagara, Elvira, Muscat, Siebel 10878 and 9110, Pinot Chardonnay, Pinot Noir, and many more. In addition, wines are made in such Canadian cities as Victoria, Kelowna, London, Moncton, out of honey, loganberries, strawberries, blueberries and with infusions of herbs. It isn't surprising that there is such a variety of taste sensations, nor that there are so many adjectives to describe them.

CHAPTER TWO

Wine Is Happiness

CANADIAN wines are relatively young but already they been associated with the happy moments of this country's life. They have been used to bless many a bride and toast wedded couples on their 50th anniversary; they have been used for christening parties, bar mitzvahs, and for sealing engagements. They have launched naval vessels and runabout dinghies. They have appeared from clandestine hampers and car trunks for picnics in spring woods or alfresco meals at autumnal horse shows. Canadian wine has honored the university graduate and the service club luncheon speaker. It is in thousands of homes and restaurants and hotels for Christmas dinners and New Year's parties. Canadian wine even helped mark Canada's Centennial Year.

The little Ontario town of Ingersoll is renowned for its cheese. When 1967, centennial year, came along, the people of Ingersoll wanted to mark the birthday by using their own product, but they couldn't simply eat cheese, so they decided on a wine and cheese party in the town arena. Four hundred and fifty were expected; 750 turned up and waited in line to get into the party. The event was repeated the following year when more than 1,200 drank wine and ate cheese. Again the celebration was held in 1969; this time 2,000 were present. This is Canada's largest regular wine and cheese party, but parties for 500 are not uncommon. Professional associations, for example, now hold conventions where these parties have replaced the cocktail party.

The number of smaller wine and cheese parties in homes for from half a dozen to 20 guests are uncountable. They have brought the most notable single change in Canadian drinking patterns in recent times. There are so many of these parties because they are initially easy for the host and hostess to arrange, and because Canada is one of the few countries to produce both good cheese and good wine. All that is necessary is a few bottles of wine, usually dry and sweet, red and white, and a rosé or two for the women guests. In Ontario there are wine stores that will deliver these bottles along with wine glasses for the party. All that the hostess has to do is to order a cheese tray from the proliferating number of stores which now specialize in cheeses. They come with crackers, often with serviettes, a board for slicing, sometimes a cheese knife. Nothing could be simpler. The host doesn't have to be a wine specialist nor, like the cocktail party host, does he need a bar full of accessories and mixes. The hostess unwraps the cellophane, and she has herself a party.

It is once again a case of the customer being right. Cheese is the ideal food to accompany wine, especially a variety of wines. Only the most Victorian of traditionalists might say that fresh fruit is better. Saintsbury, for one, claimed that the medlar, a very bitter fruit even when ripe, was the very best companion for wines, and others of his generation regularly used to peel pears with their port.

The wine and cheese party is still usually semiformal, an "occasion" in most Canadian homes. The neighborly drinking of home-made wines is generally spontaneous.

Canadians, all 20 million men, women and children, drink two-thirds of a gallon of wine each annually. The two-thirds of a gallon average hardly makes us a wine-drinking nation in the manner of France, Portugal or Italy, where the per capita consumption in 1964 was 32.8, 30.4 and 28.0 gallons respectively. But on the other hand, we drink far more wine than the Japanese, and only slightly less than the people of the U.S.A.; in fact, if all our home-made wine were taken into account, our per capita consumption might be about the same as the Americans. While sales of Canadian-produced wines now exceeds 10 million gallons annually, it was estimated three or four years ago that half as much again was being made in the kitchens and fermenting merrily in the basements of Canadian homes.

Officially in Ontario, anyone who makes more than 100 gallons of wine is supposed to acquire a licence to do so. In recent years about 25 licences a year have been issued. Everybody from liquor control board officials to commercial winery executives know there are a lot more people making 100 gallons of wine. They only have to watch the volume of California grapes or grape juice that arrives by tank car into Canada. But as long as there is no attempt to sell homemade wines, everybody turns a blind eye.

Government officials would have to be multiplied many times to check the homes of winemakers, and the winemaking industry generally tolerates the practice in the belief that it is better to have a family exposed to wine rather than one where it is an unknown quantity. This argument may be sound. Most of the big makers of home-made wine are recent immigrants to large cities like Toronto from some of those lands where 28 and 30 gallons is the national yearly average. They are first generation Canadians. It is possible that their sons and daughters won't want to make it themselves but will buy it ready-to-serve at the nearest store. These immigrants are undoubtedly still the bulk of the home-made winemakers but there are a growing number of Canadians, frequently native-born, for whom winemaking has become a hobby.

This do-it-yourself faculty has now been made easy by the growth of specialized stores which sell all the implements of the winemaker's craft. Even department stores, while they still won't sell tobacco, offer wine presses and capping devices.

Whether born in Orillia or Oporto, Medicine Hat or Milan, home winemakers are proud and sure of their product. They like nothing better than to watch the reaction of a friend to their wine – except drinking it themselves. So the neighbour who drops in unexpectedly, the friend who visits for the evening, the relative who comes for supper, finds himself a taster and tester.

Nor should such delights be legalized out of existence. Certainly commercial winemakers don't appear to ever want it to happen, perhaps because there is a cameraderie among winemakers. This is evident in the industry itself. The Canadian Wine Institute represents nearly all the wine companies of the country, and they share their knowledge to a remarkable degree. A grape growers association, in turn, is the sounding board for individual problems; the growers and wineries meet amicably.

Maybe it all stems from vocation. There can be few tasks more rewarding than bringing a small vine cutting to fruition, and then making and drinking the wine from the grapes as most Canadian growers do. There can be little that is more satisfying than producing by trial and error, by the use of different grapes, by blending, by using the right techniques, a good wine that is multiplied thousands of times on a bottling line.

Environment certainly is a factor. The vineyard areas of the world, usually with local wineries in the heart of them, are among the most blessed. I have seen many of them: Those on the island hillsides which produce the white Capri wine of the Mediterranean; others between Haifa and Tel Aviv, which grow in what was once a malarial swamp on Israel's coastal belt; some not far from the Vienna Woods Strauss made famous; hundreds of acres, interspersed with white, Dutch-style homes around Paarl in the Cape Province of South Africa; others along the Rhine and Moselle in Germany or on the Tuscan hills near Florence; in the Finger Lakes region of New York State; north of Lisbon, spreading out from Dijon in France; near Jerez de la Frontiera in Spain; beside the Black Sea in the U.S.S.R.; between the Juras and the Alps in Switzerland.

The Niagara Peninsula and the Okanagan Valley are as happy vineyard places to visit as any, and do live up to their soubriquets of "banana belt" and "sun trap of Canada." The grape grower needs scientific data rather than a label, though, so the warmth needed to ripen the grape and to specifically increase its sugar content is measured in heat units of day-degrees over 50 degrees temperature Fahrenheit. Thus, if the temperature in a vineyard reached 77 degrees on three consecutive days, three times 27, or 81 heat units, would have been collected. The long-term yearly mean total for the months of April to October inclusive are 1900 at Okanagan Centre and 2370 at Vineland in the Niagara Peninsula. This figure is above the recording for many German vineyards. As a matter of fact, the Vineland figure exceeds that for all German slopes and is near that for Bordeaux in southwest France.

As one would expect of Canada in winter, even in these balmier regions, there is a great difference in figures compared with Europe. The lowest temperature ever recorded at Okanagan Centre was 22 degrees below zero, the lowest at Vineland 16 degrees below zero, and even at Victoria, where there is a winery and roses are expected to bloom at Christmas, the thermometer once dropped to four. Even in Europe's most northerly "wine country," Germany, such temperatures are unheard of.

These statistics do not lie as far as the Canadian vine grower is concerned. They mean that while he can plant vines that grow grapes as readily and are as productive as any in Europe because of the beneficience of his summer, they must be winterhardy.

Perhaps, then, it is appropriate that we should

look at a Canadian vineyard in mid-winter. Whether east or west, the vines are a disappointing overture. Gnarled near the root-stock because of their age with leafless lateral branches extended on wires between posts, they look skeletal, crucified. But there are footprints in the snow around them because while the plants are dormant from the beginning of December through to March of each year, the growers, muffled against the cold, carry out day after day an essential of good grape culture – pruning. As much as 90% of the vine may disappear by successive cuttings through these cold months. At the end of February or by mid-March the snows will disappear and the rains will come to wash in the chemical fertilizers and barnyard manures. Then in early May, the peculiar Canadian admixture of spring and summer bursts in these two areas, a week or two earlier than in the rest of Canada.

The Niagara Peninsula is about 40 miles long and extends from Hamilton to Niagara Falls. The Okanagan Valley fruit growing region on either side of its twin lakes is somewhat shorter. Both are magnets in May for lovers of spring beauty. In Niagara, thousands of city dwellers drive along the Queen Elizabeth Highway, or if they are wise, through the scenic sideroads of Lincoln County to see the blossoms against a blue sky and green fields. Of course, it is the spectacular peach, cherry and apple blossoms that catch their attention, but if they look between the orchards next time, they will see the thousands of acres of vines are no longer bare, but in leaf.

The grower is second to no man in admiring this wonder, but it does mean work. Sprays and powders against mildew, phylloxera, and other infestations have to be regularly applied; the ground must be hoed. In the Okanagan, water spraying begins.

Through the heat of June, July and August, the grape forms and grows in its bunches. The yeasts settle, the sugar increases. Then in September the leaves yellow slightly. By the middle of the month, and through to mid-October for different areas and different grapes, the extra local workers or transients are in the vineyards picking the crop. This is the wineries' busiest time. Grapes by the ton are poured from trucks into crushers. The fermentation begins. It is a cycle that, with few variations, has been going on for thousands of years in many parts of the world, and for 100 years, albeit at the start on a very small scale, in Canada.

I have said this all happens in the pleasanter parts of the world. Come closer to catch the mood in Canada at a vineyard and a champagne fermentation plant more than 2,000 miles apart. Growers Wine Company in Victoria is the oldest winery in British Columbia. Its grapes come from across the water. Thompson's Seedless grapes are hauled in huge trucks from California to Port Angeles, Washington. They are put on the ferry and are landed in Victoria harbor.

Now follow another strait to Vancouver, traverse the lower mainland, go up the Fraser Valley to Hope, wind through the Rockies by the Hope-Princeton Highway, proceed northwestward through the sagebrush to Penticton, follow the Okanagan lakeshore along its west shore to Kelowna, turn south on the eastern edge of the lake for a few miles through the village of Okanagan Mission.

And just beyond, 300 and more miles from the winery it serves is the Beau Sejour Vineyard, the main producer of British Columbia grapes for Growers Wine Company. It is a picture. It is the picture of a vineyard in everybody's dreams. One hundred and thirty acres of vines slope, not too steeply, down to the lake glistening in the sunshine – and this area gets more hours of sunlight a year than Hawaii. Down the road a few hundred yards, Mr. J. W. Hughes, the first major grape grower in British Columbia is still at work on his plot. He has a hoe in his hand and a straw hat on his head against the sun. He is in his 80's now. Grape growers tend to live long lives.

It is a bucolic scene. It is October. The leaves on the vines are running from yellow to blood red according to variety. All the grapes have been picked largely by elderly couples, residents of Kelowna and nearby villages. They like grape picking. No tree climbing is involved as there is with peaches and apples. It gives them a month in the sun and a little extra to add to their pensions. The pickers move down the trellises between the vine posts that are guaranteed to last 30 years. Everything is done by hand. The bunches are picked and placed in boxes that are emptied into 500-pound wooden bins. These are taken on wagons hauled by tractors down the hill to the crusher behind the home of the Schmidt family, who own the Beau Sejour Vineyard. Twelve hundred tons of grapes a year go through that crusher because the B.C. vineyards are very productive, sometimes bearing 11 tons of Himrod grapes per acre. Of course, it wasn't always like that. The juice from the crush goes off from the vineyard by truck on its journey to Victoria, or to a subsidiary company, Castle Wines in Moose Jaw. It wasn't always like that, either.

The Beau Sejour Vineyard was started in 1928 when it was a desert. It was ploughed and then planted with "cover" crops which were later ploughed under. Today Italian rye grass is still planted in the same way. It takes six to eight years to get a vineyard in B.C. into full production, and a man has to eat. So Frank Schmidt planted gladioli between his vines and for years sold bulbs to seedsmen in Winnipeg and Brandon. He also raised 10,000 chickens.

Water is the main requirement for grape growing. There is an average of only 12 inches of rain in the valley making irrigation essential. But this is expensive. The water has to be lifted 510 feet from Okanagan Lake to provide the Beau Sejour vines with eight inches of water a year. A pump now does the job at the rate of 1,600 gallons a minute, but it still takes four days to irrigate the entire vineyard – by which time it is necessary to start again; otherwise the grapes would dry out.

In the early days of Beau Sejour, all the grapes were shipped by rail. They were taken to Kelowna and made up into 35 boxcar loads each year to be sent to Victoria. Now that has changed, and the vineyards have changed with the introduction of hybrids from New York State and Ontario. And now there are automatic grafting machines for grafting new varieties onto disease-resistant stocks, and soon there may be mechanical pickers; maybe the golden days of fall when the human pickers from Kelowna bend over the vines will soon be gone. But they will have their memories, and especially of that day when they stood petrified because a group of 200-pound bears had come down from the neighboring peaks and stood before them in the vineyards, reminding them that they were in Canada, a frontier land despite its fine grapes.

Eastward through the mountain passes, down the foothills, across three prairie provinces, avoiding the thousands of lakes which are northwest Ontario, southward to Niagara, four hours by jet, three days by train, two months by wagon, is the village of Jordan. It is no Johnny-come-lately to the Canadian scene. Its museum is called The Historical Museum of the Twenty. The "Twenty" marked its distance in miles from the border, the Niagara River. It was settled in the late 18th century; its pioneers were veterans of Butler's Rangers who fought with the British in the American War of Independence. Among its early settlers were Mennonites and Huguenots seeking religious freedom. They were industrious people and Jordan became a thriving port. They were people of the land, farmers and grape growers and winemakers. The Museum at Jordan consists of three buildings and a church; all date back to early and middle 19th century. One of these is called the Vintage House because it was used by Jordan Wines Limited, one of Ontario's leading wine producers, during the grape harvest. In not-too-distant years, some of the transient workers who plied the tobacco fields, peach orchards, and vineyards as pickers, were lodged there.

Part of Jordan's large operation – its champagne plant – is a few yards from the Vintage House. Stepping into this village on a hot August morning is like taking a cool dip. There is little that is more idyllicly pastoral in Canada. The stone building in which the champagne is stored and bottled is covered with ivy. Inside there is an immediate aroma of wine that is the badge of every winery in the country. A few miles away, the acrid fumes may rise from the steel plants bordering Hamilton Bay; the smog may lie heavy over Toronto. But here, in the below-ground storage cellars the temperature is constant summer or winter, almost half-way between 50 and 60 degrees.

The Jordan Company uses the traditional bottle fermentation method for its champagne but now, because it is August, stocks are low. The holding tanks of oak and redwood, built more than 50 years ago, are full of more water than wine – hot running water to clean the insides of any crust, cold running water to swell the wood and seal leaks before they are filled with a new offering from the grapes of September.

It is a quiet time, a time to ponder. Down the road the grapes are swelling. Soon they will be brought in to the Ontario wineries. Not with the prolific yield of British Columbia, because four tons an acre is more the rule here. But then irrigation with its high costs isn't necessary. But for the moment all is peaceful, a time to open a bottle of this product of sun and soil, vine and vintner's art, before moving on to find out how it came about that grapes now grow in the Rockies and a champagne that bubbles and sparkles and pops when it is opened is made beside Lake Ontario.

CHAPTER THREE

From
Vinland Westward

THE Norsemen in their first travels to North America could have had little to console them on their miserable journeys in small vessels across the North Atlantic. It is not surprising, therefore, that they marked the finding of wild vines on this foreign land mass as a highlight, and named it Vinland. Their landfall, the archives of some U.S. universities notwithstanding, might well have been part of what today is Canada as there is no vegetative proof that they landed further south. No New England state has a native wine industry today. New York has one, but based on vines growing far inland, and although it is likely that the first wine made in North America by other than indigenous people was in one of Sir Walter Raleigh's first settled areas, these are too far south to be considered in the Vinland controversy.

Could it have been not the grape vine that these early Scandinavians found, but the blueberry? Blueberries so abound in our Maritime provinces that we now have a winery in Moncton, New Brunswick, set up basically to make wine from that berry. The Norsemen after all were a people not accustomed to the sight of the grape. In any case, grape or blueberry, it is unlikely that they found time to make the first Canadian wine. That had to wait another 500 years or so. The French, being our first settlers and a wine-drinking people, were quick to experiment: Jesuit priests usually are regarded as the actual pioneers in the use of native Canadian vines for the making of their daily drink. In Le Jeune's Relation of 1636 which deals with the Jesuits' activities, it is recorded that, "In some places there are many wild vines loaded with grapes; some have made wine of them through curiosity; I tasted it, and it seemed to me very good. Many are sure that the vine would succeed here; and, when I urged against this the rigor of the cold, they replied that the vine-stock will be safe all winter under the snow, and that in the spring it need not be feared that the vines will freeze as they do in France, because they will not sprout so early."

Unfortunately, as many vine growers were to find afterwards, optimism is not enough. Lower Canada's winters were just too cold for vineyards, and certainly, as may have been the case, for vines brought from France. Quebec has always demanded more wine than any other part of Canada because of the French-Canadian palate, but has never been able to produce a local product.

Even when the early Jesuits were still making their bold attempts there probably wasn't sufficient for sale by Jacques Boisdon, who was granted in 1648 by the Council of New France the right to become the first Quebec innkeeper. Restrictions on M. Jacques Boisdon, incidentally, may have influenced the climate of drinking in Canada through succeeding centuries. Controls were abundant even then, for his tavern had to be in a public square of Quebec City not far from the church, presumably so that the good fathers could make sure that he carried out the orders laid down to him "to prevent any unseemliness, drunkenness, blasphemy or games of chance in his house." With such proscriptions he would hardly run any risks by offering a local product, which was an unknown quantity, particularly as to potency. He had no need to, having been offered by the governing council shipment of "eight barrels gratis" from France. Presumably it was wine because he also received the right to use an already established nearby brewery. Besides, he had a monopoly. Why take chances in matters temporal when spiritual surveillance was so close?

Yet some followed the Jesuits' lead and for years small quantities of wine continued to be made for church purposes by individual missionaries. This practise is carried on, to a minute degree by some priests and members of at least one order situated north of Montreal to the present day. But there has never been a large commercial winery in the province of Quebec making wines of local grapes.

In Upper Canada, the climate was milder and the native grape vine proliferated. Even before the white man penetrated into the continent, the Seneca, Tuscarora and Cayuga Indians are believed to have annually brought a gift of grape juice to the water gods who dwelt below Niagara Falls. The ceremony was called Wisachgimi. It is probable that, allowing for distance and rate at which they travelled and that the travelling was in warm weather, the grape juice would have fermented before they reached the "altar" of the falls. It is conceivable, too, that the journey would have been a dusty one so that the Indians were sufficiently tempted to slake their throats with a portion of the "gifts."

The white man could get equally thirsty, especially after a long day's toil in the fields, so it is probable that one of the settlers not far from where the Indians made their yearly sacrifice was the first to make wine in Ontario – at least for his own use. This may have been Major David Secord, brother-in-law of the famous Laura Secord. In 1798 he was granted a parcel of land by the Crown, near what is the village of St. David's today. He deeded part of his farm to his son who in turn passed it to Porter Adams in 1857.

Mr. Adams is generally recognized as the first man to plant grapes in Ontario, but it is inconceivable that there weren't good wild vines on the Secord land, which is at the very centre of today's most productive grape area. If there were, the retired army officer would surely have tried his hand at a little home-made wine. Today, Porter Adams, is honoured by grape growers for being the first to systematically plant and cultivate vines. In 1957, 100 years later, the grape growers marketing board of Ontario conducted an unsuccessful search to find the oldest living vines in the province. John Sotheridge, it was discovered, planted his vines at Stoney Creek in 1894; Thomas Field planted his at Niagara-on-the-Lake around the turn of the century but these are not very old for Ontario. There may indeed still be grape-bearing vines that were planted 100 years ago in Canada.

Porter Adams was not, however, the first winemaker in Upper Canada, the Ontario of today. In the early 1800's a German mercenary corporal, Johann Schiller, came to Canada and settled on slopes of the Credit River about 20 miles west of York (today's city of Toronto). There he found the native labrusca vines and soon was making wine in sufficient quantity to serve to his neighbors. By 1811, four years before Waterloo, where he might have served under Blucher, Schiller's combination of Old World skill and New World growth was vested in many a bottle. He is today remembered as the "father of Canadian winemaking."

Schiller didn't have any immediate successors; the countryside was still too sparsely populated. It wasn't until the immigrant wave of the 1860's and 70's that everybody in southern Ontario seemed to be trying their hand at winemaking. By now there was a chance the wine was being prepared from grapes carefully cultivated rather than from the idiosyncratic product of a wild, rambling vine.

In 1860, a letter to the editor of the *Canadian Agriculturist* from a Port Dalhousie correspondent referred to the many German farmers of the neighborhood making large quantities of wine, some of which "resembled a good Madeira."

In the same year, John C. Kilborne, writing from Beamsville to the same editor reported, "three years ago four or five barrels of wine were grown from a single vine in one season in the township of Grimsby" and that "the wine very much resembles port." Mr. Kilborne was himself to become a noted grape grower. In the same letter, he continued, "I obtained a vine six years ago last spring, it now covers some forty square feet of trellis and I think has at least twelve hundred clusters of grapes. The wine sells in this area for one dollar and three quarters a gallon, and probably would bring more if we asked for it. At all events it is worth four times as much as the miserable stuff generally sold by our merchants under the name of wine."

By now the Niagara Peninsula was being well settled by people who were planting orchards and growing fruit bushes. It is understandable that they would find an emolument in grape growing. Interest in the crop soared to such an extent that by the mid-sixties, J. M. DeCourtenay had written two related pamphlets on the subject, both with grandiose titles. The first, printed in Quebec in 1863, was called *The Culture of the Vine and Emigration*. The second, put out in Toronto in 1866, was titled *The Canada Vine Grower: How every farmer in Canada may plant a vineyard and make his own wine*. They came a little late for some.

In 1862, the same John Kilborne to whom we have referred, won first prize of three dollars at the Provincial Exhibition held in Toronto for "best three bottles wine, made from the grape." Second prize, incidentally, was won by a judge, not of the contest, but of the courts. Six years later, exhibition officials had to change the rules because prizes were being won so frequently by commercial wine-makers. Two classes were set up – professional and amateur.

A radical change had come over Ontario wine-making. It was not only being made by professionals but it became recognized abroad. Then as now, apparently, the Canadian only made his mark when praised outside the country. The breakthrough must have been astounding to the small communities of early Canada because the recognition came in the very home of wine, France. And it couldn't have come at a more appropriate time, a few days after Canada became a nation in 1867. The *Toronto Leader*, a newspaper of the time, was positively purring when it regaled its readers on July 8 of that year with the following account:

"The French exposition has established the character of our Canadian wines. The jury on wines, which would naturally be composed of the best judges to be found in Europe, speak in very high terms of the wines sent from the Clair House Vineyards, Cooksville. They find in them a resemblance to the Beaujolais wine, which is known to be the best produced in France. They say of those wines that 'they are pure and of excellent quality, and solve the problem of Canada being able to furnish good wines.' Moreover that 'they resemble more the great French table wines than any other foreign wines they have examined, and that the fact of the wine being so "solide" as to bear the sea voyage, and the variations of heat and cold without losing anything of either its quality or limpidity, should be a question of great consideration even to our own producers.'

"This authoritative opinion of the quality of Ontario wine will do more than anything else that could possibly occur, at present, to bring this wine into general use. A new kind of wine always has to make its way against settled prejudices; and in the present case, where the supposition has been general that this was not a wine-producing country, simply because we had not measured our resources, the difficulty was greatly increased. In fact, scepticism was general; and it was not always capable of being removed by demonstrations. If any one here vouched for the quality of the wine, nothing was easier than to conclude that he was an indifferent judge or no judge at all. But this cannot be said of the jury on wines at the Paris exposition. The use of the light wine by the people is increasing every year. Probably there are now a hundred gallons of claret drunk in Toronto where one was drunk ten years ago; and this implies the general cultivation of a taste for the lighter wines, which will tell upon the demand for Canadian wine. The time will come, we hope and verily believe, when grape-growing and wine-making will be one of the principal employments of our population; and when it does come, the cause of temperance will be advanced to a degree which could be reached by no other process."

The wine which won such praise came from vines supplied to the Clair House Vineyards by the Mr. (sometimes referred to as Count) DeCourtenay who had written pamphlets on grape culture. He, like Schiller and Kilborne was one of the men most responsible for the rapid early growth of the wine industry in Canada. Alas, the claret demands by Torontonians didn't continue to increase a hundredfold each ten years. The *Toronto Leader* soon published its last edition, and eventually the Clair House Vineyards, which had brought such honor to Cooksville, Ontario and Canada, faded from the scene.

The small grape growers were of sterner stuff.

Already in 1866, the Hon. Mr. Justice Logie, in his capacity as president of the Upper Canada Fruit Growers' Association had sounded the clarion call at the annual meeting in Hamilton: "The progress already made should stimulate all engaged in the cultivation of the grape to increased effort."

Everyone was willing to take a crack. In a letter to the *Canada Farmer,* it was reported that "a company of gentlemen from Kentucky, who have been in the grape business for 14 years, have purchased a farm on Pelee Island and planted 30 acres this spring, and intend to plant 20 acres next spring."

Every school child today learns that the spur of Pelee Island, jutting out into Lake Erie, provides Canada with at least a few square miles on the same latitude as northern California. Since the earlier part of this century this peninsula has been associated with the name of Jack Miner and his efforts to provide a refuge for migratory birds. But long before the Canadian geese came, there was a surprising vineyard experiment there.

Sandusky, Ohio, almost directly south across the lake from Pelee, is one of the oldest winemaking centres in the U.S.A. By 1860, Catawba grapes were being grown successfully on Kelley's Island, 12 miles south of Pelee. Five years later, just after the American Civil War, D. J. Williams of Kentucky visited Pelee. Perhaps he realized the time was not fortuitous for further development of land, as his country was still trying to heal its battle scars. To travel from Kentucky north to Canada, he would probably have passed through Sandusky, and seen what could be accomplished with local grapes or he may have heard of the plantings at Kelley's Island near Pelee.

Williams was obviously impressed by the northern experiments and the next year, 1866, he returned to Pelee with two other southerners. Thomas Williams and Thaddeus Smith, to start the first winery on the peninsula. They formed a company, bought the land referred to by the writer to the *Canada Farmer* and planted their first vines.

As the good farmer raises his barn before his home, so does the good vintner by putting down a cellar before thinking of habitation. The Williams' and Smith actually dug their wine cellar into the rock — 12 feet deep, 40 feet wide and 60 feet long — and only then built a stone house on top of it. It must have been a busy year. Twelve months later, Thaddeus Smith returned to the South for his family and moved them into the aptly named "Vin Villa" he had helped build.

Meanwhile, Smith and the Williams' acquired neighbours; in 1866 two Englishmen, Edward and John Wardroper moved into Pelee, bought 15 acres, and also started a vineyard.

In the year D. J. Williams first saw Pelee and recognized its possibilities, J. S. Hamilton's name was added to the honor roll of graduates of the grammar school in Brantford, Ontario. Young Hamilton must have been industrious, ambitions and thrifty. He went to work as a clerk in a Brantford store and managed to save $1,000, no mean feat in that job in that century. As soon as he had made his first thousand, Hamilton started his own grocery business. Such businesses, then and since in Canada, have often been the "Open Sesame" to the wine business. In 1871, the same year he opened his store, he received a royal charter to sell both wine and liquor. It was a move that played an important part in the creation of 20 Canadian winemaking companies.

Three years later, Hamilton met Thaddeus Smith, whose Pelee vineyards were now producing four to five tons of Delaware and Catawba grapes an acre, which is still a good yield for Ontario vineyards. Hamilton saw the grapes, tasted the wine, and decided it needed marketing. He sought customers and, looking across the water from the vineyard, it was obvious they had to be in the U.S.A. with its rapidly growing population. It was the nearest point, there were no tariff walls – and soon Vin Villa wines were being widely sold in many of the eastern States.

However, J. S. Hamilton, later to become a member of the first city council of Brantford and to serve 26 years in the Dufferin Rifles where he attained the rank of major, was pre-eminently a Canadian. In business he certainly wouldn't neglect his own country and so he set about selling the wines of Pelee throughout southern Ontario and into Quebec.

Among the later companies he created were the J. S. Hamilton Company and the Pelee Island Wines and Vineyards Company. The first of these was in Brantford, a much more suitable centre for marketing in Canada than Pelee, especially as lake boats could bring the casks of matured wine to the city for bottling. These boats only met their match many years later when the Pelee Island winemaking operations were closed entirely in favor of Brantford. Then, it became much too awkward to send the huge storage casks from the Pelee cellars as deck cargo, so the casks were emptied and then floated in Lake Erie. A tug took them in tow, pulling them eastward through the lake and up the Grand River to a point near the new winery where they were then rolled ashore and installed.

However, the sight of a line of wine casks bobbing like barges on the Great Lakes is comparatively recent history. Back in the 1860's and 70's, winemaking was still very much an individual affair, a matter of single-cask families. A farmer's letter written in 1859 recounts how he "sold 100 gallons of champagne to one person who speaks highly of it and I bottled a cask for home consumption which is universally liked."

And ten years later the writer of an article in an agricultural periodical refers to the wines of Henry Bauer, a native of Hamilton, as made from the Clinton grape, mixed with about one-third of Oporto "and it is a very beautiful red wine, in flavour much resembling the red wines of Hungary."

It is easy to imagine such "tastings." They would not have been methodical and professional in the modern sense, but convivial occasions in the farmhouses of the Niagara Peninsula on wintry evenings – and beyond, because there is considerable evidence of home grape growing for winemaking through much of southern Ontario at that time, and particularly in the counties stretching between Lakes Huron and Erie, and along the north shore of Lake Ontario as far east as Kingston. The individual makers would proudly bring out their bottles from the cellar, or in the case of newly arrived immigrants from Europe, possibly pour out a jug from a cask. The guests would sip and sniff and mentally note whether it was better or worse than so-and-so at a neighboring farm had offered them a couple of nights before. Then there would be talk, a lot of it about wine; and more wine and more talk, with an even greater proportion on the merits of wine, for that is the custom of wine drinkers.

If there was debate about the "ends" there was more about the "means" in 19th-century Canada. A fruit growers' association had been formed in 1858 and was well enough known ten years later to be receiving favors; the president, in his annual address in Hamilton was able to conclude with "the manager of the Great Western Railway, with his usual liberality, has extended to members the privilege of travelling to and from the next meeting, to be holden in St. Catherines, at reduced fares."

This was but innocent "payola." Grapes and their culture were increasingly the reason for such meetings. In 1868, for example, W. Sanderson from Brantford was reporting that "grapes are claiming a large share of attention and that they will be planted out here for a few years to come . . . that Hartford Progress is not generally liked . . . and Delawares are coming gradually forward and stand first on the list as to quality."

At the same time, Z. B. Lewis, a Welland County man, claimed that "grapes appear to be the crop of this year . . . all the vineyards are loaded, the principal varieties being Concord, Delaware, Clinton, Diana and Isabella . . . speculators are offering four cents a pound, and some five cents, for the whole crop for shipment."

37

W. H. Mills, the association president for that year, waxed considerably more eloquent on the subject. In presenting a paper on the hybridizing of grapes, he began, "There is no practice more fascinating and instructive in the whole range of horticultural experience than that of producing new varieties by the art of hybridizing." It made him comprehend, he said, "that beautiful expression, 'As it was in the beginning, is now, and ever shall be,'" an unfathomable piece of logic which could have been produced by drinking heavily of wine from a hybridized grape while writing his report.

There was no denying though it was a good year for grapes. M. Y. Keating, of Louth in the County of Lincoln, said they were almost the only exception to the general failure of fruits, "the vines having stood the winter well."

It wasn't only the winter that could threaten. Many were reporting that grapes, like any other fruit or vegetable, attracted pests. These, before the days of sprays and insecticides, had to be picked off the vines by hand. At least it allowed a closer look so that one grower was able to practically romanticize, "The grape vine flea beetle (Haltica chalybea) is a very pretty beetle varying in color from steel blue to green."

1868, Canada was one year old: Pests were in the vineyards but yields were generally good; the laborers on the farms of southern Ontario were earning 75 cents to $1.25 a day plus board, but up to $2 a day at harvest (and presumably grape-picking) time; flour costing $1 to $6 a barrel of 200 pounds; "butcher meat" was $5 to $7 a hundredweight; speculators were offering 4 cents a pound for grapes.

In this infancy of a nation, individual farmers

were proud of their few trellises of vines and a few years later those rows had spread to acres, and there were American newspapermen ready to bolster the pride.

One hundred years after the Declaration of Independence, the Americans decided to celebrate with a grand centennial exhibition in Philadelphia; Ontario sent a major display of grapes. The range showed how far viticulture had advanced, the varieties including White Chasselas, Black Hamburg, Creveling, Lindley, Salem, Wilder, Sweet Water, Rebecca, Maxatawney, Tokalon, Merrimack, as well as the better-known Concords and Delawares.

The *New York Graphic* reporter saw these clusters and promptly wrote. "Probably the finest show of various fruit is made by the Fruit Growers' Association of Ontario, Canada." The association's secretary, writing to the commissioner of agriculture for the province later added his assessment, "Our display of grapes was the most complete of any. Our specimens were as fine in appearance as those shown from climates supposed to be more favored than ours. No state in the union displayed as exhaustive a collection."

The agricultural commissioner must have been a patient man. Each year the fruit growers sent him a printed report that ran to 100 pages or more. No wonder! One includes an entire debate at one meeting, in the manner of "Hansard," when a Colonel McGill presented a paper on his experiences as a grape grower at Oshawa. After telling how he laid out the vines and how he got the best bunches (where the foliage was the densest) he made the mistake of declaring in no uncertain manner that "the

Concord is the grape for the people of this part of Ontario." Several association members then jumped up to vociferously deny this and put forward their own favourites. One can imagine the scene: the colonel bristling and the other farmers, neck veins bulging as they bawled out the names – all different – of one-and-only grape varieties. Fortunately, the mayor of Trenton managed to make his voice heard and invited them all to supper. Nevertheless, the association members were not to be so easily deterred. Immediately after the pleasant intermission, rested and fortified, they returned to the fray. Words like Adirondac, Lady, Concord, Worden were spilled out, but as usual no unanimous decision was reached as to which was Canada's best wine grape, and there hasn't been to this day.

CHAPTER FOUR

Cottage Craft To Industry

H. L. MENCKEN, that great American wit and "wet" once said, "All the great villainies of history have been perpetrated by sober men, and chiefly by teetotallers." He must have had in mind that enormous social disaster, Prohibition, which ran from 1920 to 1933 in the U.S.A., but started earlier and ended earlier in Canada.

This was the attempt, as far as the United States government was concerned, to convert overnight 100 million people who had normally consumed 2,000 million gallons of alcoholic beverages each year into total abstainers. As a federal inquiry was later to dryly observe, "This was certainly an ambitious undertaking for any government."

In the United States, Prohibition brought large numbers of young women in contact with hard liquor for the first time, promoted back seat and hotel room drinking, introduced police corruption on a large scale, and certainly greatly increased crime. It would be exaggerating to claim consequences so far reaching in Canada, but the misguided endeavors of the misnamed temperance lobbies resulted in increased drunkeness and crime.

In particular, Prohibition in Canada spawned through a peculiar legal convolution, the creation of numerous dubious wineries. These made up what one of today's leading winemakers describes as a "rot-gut industry." There are many who agree with his definition. Prohibition, more than anything else, introduced the word "wino" into the Canadian language, thus denigrating all Canadian wine in the eyes of the public for at least a generation. Prohibition changed a combination of good husbandry and gentle craft into a monster whose products were so poor that it seemed bent on a form of mass suicide. Only by the skin of our teeth do we have Canadian wines today – prohibition, as we shall later discover in the book, almost dealt the death-blow.

Back in the 1870's and '80's, there was nothing that could be termed a winemaking industry. Although there were small winemaking companies as far north as Renfrew in the Ottawa Valley, most autumnal winemaking efforts were scattered and small. However, seeds of the industry – even of the industry of today which sells more than ten million gallons of wine each year – were being planted. Not only had J. S. Hamilton established his connections with Pelee but in 1873, George Barnes started a winery at St. Catharines. Titles were as prodigious as sermons in that Victorian era, so he called his company the Ontario Grape Growing and Wine Manufacturing Company, Limited. Today it still exists in St. Catharines, still with its own vineyards adjacent to the still-productive winery. Now it is simply called Barnes Wines and is the oldest wine company in Canada.

A year after George Barnes' beginning, Thomas Bright with a partner, F. A. Shirriff, started a winery in Toronto. Sixteen years later, they moved to the outskirts of what now is the city of Niagara Falls, building there a two-storey structure in which they could age 50,000 gallons of wine. That "cellar" still exists too, if only as a minute part of Brights present-day modern plant where more than seven million gallons of wine can be stored. Thomas Bright could hardly have envisioned what a considerable step he was taking. By the turn of the century, the Niagara Falls Wine Company as it was then known was selling more than its original capacity to Canadians; by 1924, Brights had the first production line in the Canadian wine industry; by 1933, after successive expansions, the wine cellars were holding four million gallons, making them the largest privately owned wine cellars in the world.

Brights move to Niagara Falls from Toronto was part of a centralization of grape growing and winemaking which proceeded in the last two decades of the 19th century. Although this was the "age of rail," it was necessary for any winery to be close to its source of supply. Conversely, Canada then wasn't urbanized as it is today. Toronto was a relatively small, compact city. The market for wine was as likely to be the individual rural dweller or the inhabitants of a succession of tiny villages and small towns as the few "city slickers" of Toronto, Kingston or London. Already it had been found that the ideal situation for any mass growing of grapes for commercial purposes was through the wind-sheltered, water-warmed Niagara Peninsula.

In the 1880's, growers like Theodore Girardot of Sandwich in southwest Ontario could still report they were manufacturing wine for commercial purposes at a selling price of $1 a gallon, and vinophiles like John Hoskin, Q.C., of Toronto could condemn the Concord grape for winemaking, but the winds of change had already begun to alter the course of the grape growing industry. The climate of Niagara, and the readiness with which the Concord agreed with it, meant that more and more farmers were buying land there and planting larger numbers of Concord vines. Immigration, too, played its part. Upper Canada was now Ontario and the new name was being passed from mouth to mouth in Britain and parts of continental Europe. The immigrants began pouring in – if they had an agricultural background they would seek good soil, and if they came from a temperate climate they headed for a similar climate – the Niagara Peninsula was often their choice.

In 1881, just over 2,000 acres of Ontario was being used for grape growing, with not one county having more than 275 acres. The total production of grapes was three- and-a-half million pounds. Ten years later the acreage had doubled, and the production tripled. Four counties – Essex, in the extreme southwest tip of the province, and Lincoln, Welland and Wentworth, all in the Niagara Peninsula – accounted for more than 70% of this acreage. The pendulum was to swing even farther with the acreages in the Niagara counties increasing each year and those in Essex declining so that by the 1920's there were only 26 acres of grapes left there compared with more than 1,000 of 30 years earlier. But those 26 acres were larger than all the grape growing lands in the rest of Canada. So predominant was Ontario in grape culture in 1921 that all but 23 acres were listed in this single province.

Although the Niagara variety of grape was much advertised for the making of white wine, each vine cost $1.25 as long ago as 1882 and this would have been a deterrent even if the Concord wasn't generally more hardy in Winter. Thus it was that this blue grape gradually became so popular as to account for 70% of all grape production and its rich, red juice, in those still unscientific days was responsible for the predominance of red wines.

Science had made its first faltering step when a professor of chemistry at the University of Toronto, Dr. Croft, analysed a couple of wines of the Clair House Vineyards shortly after it had won renown in Paris. A bottle of white was reported to contain $8\frac{9}{10}\%$ of absolute alcohol while a red had 13%. Dr. Croft undoubtedly drank both bottles because his findings are more poetic than analytical. The white he described as being a "pure and wholesome summer wine" and the red as having "an exceedingly pleasant taste."

The writing of more prosaic reports had to await the creation of the Ontario Horticultural Station at Vineland, a village in the heart of the Niagara Peninsula. Much will be written about the efforts made by the scientists and horticulturists there during this century to aid the development of good Canadian grapes and wines. Suffice it now to point out that since 1913, their work has been along three main avenues – the testing of new varieties from all parts of the world, hybridizing varieties to suit them to Ontario conditions, and research to improve grape growing methods. They have grown and inspected tens of thousands of vines and written thousands of reports on the chemical analysis of grapes and wines. It is to their honor that, despite their labs, their white coats, their concern with formulae and volumetric densities, they have been able to bridge the gap of the "two cultures" which so exercised Sir Charles Snow, and have retained an almost lyrical love of the grape and the wine it produces.

After Barnes and Brights, licences were to be issued to eight more wineries before September, 1916 in Ontario. In less than 11 succeeding years, another 33 wineries were started. This was the indirect result of Prohibition.

When the Ontario Temperance Act was introduced, the sale of all alcoholic beverages, except for medical purposes became illegal. However, there was a notable flaw and it is remarkable that the politicians of the day, looking to the rural vote, forgot. They soon found out about it. The grape growers of the Niagara Peninsula, and most notably from three constituencies, descended upon the members of the provincial legislature with wrath: "Where," they asked, "are we going to sell our grapes?" So it was that wine, and only wine made in Ontario, became the only legal alcoholic drink that could be sold in the province until 1927.

But there were strings attached, the most notable one being that the wine could only be sold at a single outlet attached to each individual winery. And one other: The "temperance" government, dominated by the "temperance" movement, considered that the best and only way to maintain temperance was to pass an extraordinary edict that these winery outlets should not be allowed to sell to any one cutsomer at any one time less than a five gallon keg of wine, or, if preferred, a case containing no fewer than 12 bottles. Man would be hardly human if in this alice in crazyland situation he hadn't wanted to exploit his fellow man a little by providing him with a drink, so the winery rush started with all the fervor of a Klondike.

It so happened that, at the time, one of the Welland Canals was being constructed, roads were being built, railway lines laid – all in the Niagara Peninsula. Many of the workers on these projects were Italians and others from Europe who drank wine with their meals. There they were working hard by luscious vineyards thinking about how to get some wine and, as a corollary, how to make it. In somewhat shorter time than it takes to spell out that four-letter word, "vino," they had decided on their basements. Thus it came about that many of the wineries of the Prohibition era in Canada were started in basements – and garages – and the backs of grocery stores.

Licences were applied for, and handed out by the Board of Liquor Commissioners to keep the grape growers happy, and, in many instances, wineries were started with the crudest of equipment. There was virtually no inspection, no questions and no food and drug act controls – but there was a large, thirsty market waiting. The market was not only in Canada. The U.S.A. had its Prohibition, too, so Canadian wine was finding its way to customers other than through the single outlet attached to the winery. For instance, a remarkable quantity in those years, judging by the shipping manifests, was exported to the islands of St. Pierre and Miquelon, off the coast of Newfoundland. Nobody quite knows why because they have tiny populations, are French possessions, and have always drunk the wines of their homeland. The common consensus is that somebody managed to steer the cargoes intended for these islands to Buffalo and Detroit and points west rather than east.

A welcome supply to the good American neighbors who were in somewhat direr straits than Canadians because sale of native wine wasn't legal in their country, was ever forthcoming because of another simple ruse – many of the new-found Canadian wineries were conveniently located near the banks of the Welland Canal. This is not the present canal; nevertheless its predecessor was a very busy shipping channel equipped with locks that necessitated ships tying up to await passage. While a ship is hawsered to a bollard, particularly at night, a surprising number of casks of wine can be rolled a few hundred yards to find their way into its hold. These activities of a few rugged individualists, as those entrepreneurs are often referred to today, took care of the U.S. market.

There was also the matter of the domestic market. Some of the winemakers of the Niagara Peninsula didn't even apply for licences. They simply made as much as they could in their basements and became, not to put too fine a point on it, backdoor bootleggers. Others ran stores and sold only medicated wines – legally. It was also legal, as it has been pointed out, to sell wine from one outlet – the premises of the winery. The only trouble was that if the winery was in the Niagara Peninsula, the customers for cities like Toronto had to face a journey of 50 to 80 miles each way to acquire their five gallons or cases of 12; this was before cars were common. It really meant an all-day, if not weekend, trip. So, in the age-old logistical manner of business, the supplier had to go to the customer. Bootleggers abounded to provide this service. And, in addition, the wineries moved away from the source of supply of grapes. Not only were outlets started in Toronto, but in Hamilton, Windsor, and Fort William. One outlet in a northern Ontario town was actually located in a dairy, which at least might have provided the customer with the protection of pasteurized wine.

The sudden deployment of the industry meant that the grapes, in many cases, had to travel hundreds of miles to the wineries. Not that the tonnage which travelled this distance would have been heavy. Eventually, when order was restored after the days of Prohibition it was found that not infrequently 600 gallons of wine had been produced from a ton of grapes. This is more than twice the legal limit now, and has evinced the comment that if just one more gallon of water had been added, it wouldn't have been wine.

There were many additives without that extra gallon of water. In the post-mortem period, it was found that because so much water was added to the wine dyes had to be added to colour the water to make it look like wine. The additions of colourings is not unknown to the food industry, and the use of vegetable dyes is common for this purpose throughout the world. The only trouble is that some of the wineries of the 1920's used coal tar dyes, even formaldehyde. There, too, was another reason why the product became so diluted. Many of the new winemakers could only obtain second-hand equipment such as casks from the U.S.A. This meant the equipment was calibrated, if calibrated at all, in U.S. gallons, but the measure in Canada is based on the larger Imperial gallon. The neophyte winemakers were simply confused by this, if they knew – and some undoubtedly didn't. The easiest solution was for everybody to remain ignorant.

Not all the wineries of this weird decade should, however, be thrown into the same low classification. We have noted that a firm like Brights was leading the way with such revolutionary developments as the first bottling line in Canada. Other firms, some of them today's major producers, were started then including the Jordan Wine Company, the London Winery, and the Turner Wine Company.

Turner Wine Company was started by a man with the reputation of "looking like a preacher and swearing like a trooper." The company was started in 1920, almost midway through the Prohibition period. The pulpit-barracks room dichotomy per-sonified in this one man was common in those years. Thus, in the strong temperance area of Saltfleet Township near Hamilton, many farmers refused to sell their grapes for winemaking, while a few miles down the road other growers would demand higher prices for badly blemished grapes which normally would have been considered too poor for wine-making.

The wine sold during Prohibition was usually red or as it was often called, a "port type," the ratio being nearly five to one in favour of red over white wine. The Concord grape filled the need. As more wineries opened and the public thirst grew, prices soared so that some growers were eventually getting

$120 a ton for their grapes, a figure they weren't to receive again until 40 years later.

What was the wine like in those ugly days? In the view of Adhemar F. de Chaunac, a courtly gentleman who came from Europe to subsequently become Brights winemaker, the red was "sweet," the white was "undrinkable." Some might say half of his assessment was correct, the other half charitable.

Perhaps even the average Canadian had come to the same conclusion. It wouldn't be true to say that he alone was responsible for the repeal of Prohibition but he was getting tired, by the later 1920's, of getting his hard liquor and beer by illegal methods and by buying wine that was inferior. The politicians, too, were becoming disturbed. Despite all the high hopes for the temperance movement, all their little tracts handed out to school children through such organizations as the Little Temperance League, it was becoming obvious that Dad (and increasingly, now, Mum) would continue to drink. And more people were concerned at the newspaper reports of the crime associated with bootlegging in the U.S.A. And some even thought far enough ahead to see that by making alcoholic beverages illegal a valuable source of tax revenue was being lost.

Now, at last, all but the "hard core" abstention groups, within and outside the churches, realized that perhaps drinking could be moderated by lifting the ban. The accent was put on "control" rather than "forbid" and in 1927, Ontario, following most of the other provinces, introduced its Liquor Control Act.

Prohibition had ended. In its place, the various

governments of Canada for the first time moved directly into the field of alcoholic drinks demanding taxes but in exchange controlling the quality of the products offered the customer. There was no jubilation at the change. Prohibition ignominiously died but there was no vast drunken wake to mark its passing. Especially was there no rejoicing by the men given the task of succoring the wine industry. They faced an unenviable task: "Operation Clean-up."

CHAPTER FIVE

The Renaissance

TODAY there are 51 stores selling nothing but wine throughout Ontario. They are owned by the wine companies of the province, ranging from Brights, which has 14, to others which have only a couple.

The reason why there are 51 is that when the task of resuscitating the wine industry started, 51 licences were issued to wineries; each was allowed one store. Actually, there is a minor mystery here because there was believed to have been a 52nd licence issued to a winery in Belleville but, during the handover from the old Board of Liquor Commissioners to the newly formed Liquor Control Board in the late 1920's the record of this licence was mislaid and has never been found.

The control of the 51 wine stores of today by eight wine companies instead of more than six times that number of companies stems directly from an intensive plan carried out before the Second World War to put the Ontario wine industry, which was still essentially the entire Canadian wine industry, on a stable base so that it might survive.

This wasn't to be survival at the expense of the wine drinker; the public had to be protected – indeed, demanded it. With the coming of The Liquor Control Act, government stores, as well as those attached to the wineries, were allowed to sell Canadian wines. Immediately protests started flooding in; bottles of wine were vinegary, full of sediment, occasionally holding foreign matter. The Liquor Control Board of Ontario decided to assess the entire winemaking procedures of the province. It moved fast, first bringing in a ruling that no wine could contain more than one part in 400 of volatile acid. This was still a high ratio and meant that a trace of vinegar could still be tasted. But it immediately put half the fly-by-night, so-called winemakers of the twenties out of business.

This wasn't a very subtle expedient but the government and its agency dared not take a more direct approach. The Depression was hitting the farmer as much as the city dweller. Concord grape prices had plummetted to $12 a ton. Wine was selling at 30 cents a bottle in the liquor stores. The backroom winemakers of Niagara couldn't be legislated out of their livelihoods.

Still, the number of wineries was halved again. This time it was because of a school, started under the aegis of Sir Henry Drayton, a former national minister of finance who had become head of Ontario's liquor board. The school, which ran for two years, was intended to teach people in the wine industry how to make wine. It was taught in English, but many of those attending the school couldn't write English; some couldn't speak it. They quickly became "drop outs" and switched from winemaking to some other vocation.

It was the old evolutionary process of survival of the fittest but the new changing standards weren't welcomed on all scores. It sadly reduced, for example, the number of anecdotes about the mysterious wines produced during Prohibition and for a few years thereafter. It was not unknown, for instance, that some of these poor wines would re-ferment in the bottle. One liquor store vendor in Ganonoque, near Kingston, reported testily to his Toronto headquarters on the effects on his morale of this peculiar phenomenon. He would be doing his bookwork quietly at night in the store when a bottle would explode, frightening him out of his skin. He wanted to know what he should do, and was advised to return the wine to the winery. When no further word was forthcoming, headquarters asked the disconcerted vendor the reason. The vendor explained that one day a bottle had exploded when an American visitor was in the store, who maintained it must be champagne, and thinking he was getting a bargain, bought all five- and a-half cases of the poor wine.

There also was the wine called Catawba, one of the cheapest sold in Canada and called by most of the people who drank it "cat-a-waba." It shouldn't be mistaken for the product of the Catawba grape, from which good champagne is regularly made. Particularly as one member of the Ontario Legislature once referred to it as "block and tackle," an appelation he said it deserved because you "drink a bottle, run a block, and are prepared to tackle anyone."

The Liquor Control Board couldn't be expected

to support legends. As the 1930's proceeded, it took even sterner measures. The degree of volatile acid in the wines was further reduced by law so that it could no longer be distinguished. Action was also started to eliminate the medicated and tonic wine business. Some store owners who had made this wine branched out into the regular wine business; others were still doing a considerable trade with their own products across grocery store counters when wine was obtainable in liquor stores. The Liquor Control Board scratched its collective head and came up with a novel solution: It decreed it was permissible to sell these "medications" if a certain additive was put in the wine. As the additive induced vomiting if the wine was taken in large quantities, the whole business quickly collapsed.

This, while original, was a simple problem compared with the economic crisis which suddenly developed for the now-remaining wine industry. The introduction of wine selling at liquor stores created a shift in the buying pattern from the wine stores attached to wineries; the Depression was having an overall adverse effect on wine sales anyhow, and the population of Canada was filtering towards the cities and away from the smaller centres of the Niagara Peninsula. So it was first decided that the surviving sounder wineries could buy out those which had already foundered or appeared about to do so. The buying prices had to be fair, and were subject to the approval of the liquor board. In most cases, the equipment, good will and name of the seller were worthless. What was valuable was the store attached to the winery. In most cases, the wineries were bought for $5,000 to $10,000 each; the equipment was scrapped and wine stocks were sent to a

distillery to make grape spirit, but the buyer did get the attached wine outlet which could start business again selling the new owner's products. For the arithmetically minded, it is thus possible to know precisely how many wineries extant companies bought out. As has been mentioned, Brights have 14 stores, one of which was attached originally to their Niagara Falls plant; therefore, they bought 13 other wineries.

The next step was to move these stores to the market-place and so legislation was also introduced permitting the wineries to transfer their outlets to the larger urban centres from the Niagara district.

With all of these measures, the survivors were still faced with those doom-laden days of the Depression. The prairie farmer who was paid a few cents a bushel for his wheat was hardly likely to wine and dine. In the cities, the terms "bread line" and "soup kitchen" provided a hint of what was a fairly universal diet.

Grape growers especially suffered. Some drove 200 and 300 miles north with stake trucks laden with grapes which, if they were lucky, they could sell to home-made winemakers at $12 a ton. This decade in the wine business was every bit as much a time of "rugged individualists" as the decade before.

Frank Cooper is an example of the breed. He was the son of a small storekeeper in Welland, a Ukrainian by birth who liked his wine and who, in 1919, bought a grape crusher to make it. Frank was brought up with the aroma of fermenting grapes in his nostrils. In his teens he drove the family truck to farms, bought grapes at $12 to $15 a ton and re-sold them to anyone who wanted to make wine at

$1 a ton profit – purchasers were allowed to borrow the family crusher. Eventually, the man who was to become Frank Cooper's father-in-law received a licence to start a winery in the last year of Prohibition. Although the firm had an asset which few could match in Paul Rosenberg, a fifth-generation German winemaker, it was an inauspicious moment to start a winery. The company staggered along with its single attached store. Cooper's wife used to serve there and help with the bookkeeping.

The problems weren't eased during the Second World War. Sugar and bottles were rationed, only part-time employees could be found; it took a year to obtain bottle caps. Yet Frank Cooper, in 1945, became a full-time winemaker and struggled on with the help of two men. In that year he produced only 900 bottles of wine a day; when he sold his company in 1964, it was producing 450 cases of wine a day. To achieve this only modest mark in the context of the whole Canadian industry, he started off by making even the boxes in which the grapes were collected from scrap wood which came into Welland protecting shipments of glass.

Problems were a daily diet. Once, the fermentation tanks holding 35,000 gallons of wine in his small plant started going out of control because of a spell of hot weather. Frank Cooper called upon his brother-in-law, who was in the ice business to make a delivery while he busied himself cutting large holes in the roof of the winery. Tongs dragged the chunks of ice up the pitch of the roof. Frank, like a crane director, stood below. The ice fell through, and eventually quelled the volcanic vats.

At least one Hungarian was a temporary ingredient of another vat. Immigrants who lived locally were often helpers at vintage time, working on the crush of the grapes. Their pay was 25 cents an hour plus all the wine they could drink. It was the latter part of this remuneration which once overcame a worker and had him dog paddling in wine when he tumbled into a vat.

Limitation of the amount of water added to the grape juice, control of acidity, a new accent on hygiene, certainly bettered the wines of the thirties. The basic taste, however, did not change because most of the wines were made from the dark red, sweet Concord grape.

In 1931, fortification of wines with spirit made from native grapes was allowed, helping the grower sell more grapes, aiding the maker who wanted a means to preserve his wines, and benefiting the customer who wanted ports and sherries with alcoholic content as high as their European counterparts. These fortified wines were immediately popular, accounting for 30% of all sales which were reduced because after reaching three- and a-half million gallons in 1930, the Depression continued to force down annual consumption through the succeeding years.

Canadian wine was still shackled, with triple chains. To the Women's Christian Temperance Union and the many they persistently influenced, wine was a member of an unholy trinity along with demon rum and evil old John Barleycorn – an enemy of the people, a very devilhead. To the weak, the embittered, the defeated, the down-and-out, it was a release. For the majority, who in those impecunious years could hardly be called a middle class, it was a luxury. It would have been a brave prophet to then forsee that Canadian wines could become an elegant, acceptable condition of life attainable by all within a quarter century.

There were a few, a very few, working quietly, methodically determined in this nadir of economic circumstances that wine could be changed, improved, sold. Some were businessmen with faith in their own abilities and their country. They controlled or acquired the residue of the Prohibition era wine industry. They could not make vast changes in a season, hardly in the decade that has deserved its opprobrious "dirty." They could only set course.

There were others who did not look upon wine as a luxury. In the homelands from which they had come, wine – table wine of good quality but low average alcoholic content – was the daily beverage with meals for every family. They were the grape breeders, the chemists, the winemakers. For them the whole drinking climate must have been alien. Wine to them and their ancestors came from the pleasure glass on weekdays, the altar cup on Sundays, and the twain had long been rationalized. Wine to them was as natural as air or bread or animals in the barn. In Canada it was a dirty word. Many must have come, seen, and quickly returned. Others despaired, stayed, but fought over the years for a better product, and especially a better table wine to grace the food of what was to become the second richest country on earth.

One of these immigrants was Adhemar de Chaunac, ultimately to become winemaker for the nation's largest winery. He may be classed as a true representative of the small elite bound to give Canada better wines. Like DeCourtenay who had acted as such a spur to better native wines when the nation was still unjoined by rail, de Chaunac proudly showed his ethnic origins in his name. Pride, however, often has to bow to compromise. Previous tests had shown the inability of the vinifera grape vines of Burgundy or Rhine to adapt to the Canadian soil; only man had done that. But obviously to de Chaunac and his contemporaries, the heavy reliance on the Concord would never better the wines.

So vines were brought in from New York State, with its fairly similar, slightly more severe, climatic conditions. Brights, with its large test plot; the Vineland station; other wineries of the peninsula were willing to experiment. The Delaware, Elvira, President, Seneca, and Agawam grape breeds all grew successfully, were winter hardy, brought distinctive tastes to wine. Blending of wines was tried using a mixture of juices from different varieties and the quality of wines improved. They were tasted and found acceptable by the last tasters, the public. Sales shot up; an industry was reborn.

None of the work of 35 years came easy. For every vine of a variety that succeeded, ten or 100 might have died. There were notable successes; the Agawam grape was found to marry well with the juice of others. Today this blend results in the Manor St. Davids white wine which sells hundreds of thousands of bottles yearly.

Yet when de Chaunac thought a series of his early experiments had resulted in a superior wine, he was only allowed to make it in a 500-gallon vat. Failing to find one available, he, with some temerity, decided to make 1,000 gallons. There are probably a few home-made winemakers now who wouldn't flinch at that supply for their personal use.

The Second World War neither aided the winery nor the experimenter. The sources of European vines were cut off; even the shipment from the U.S. had to take last transportation rights after arms, troops and much else. In any case, there were difficulties with many of the New York State varieties. They were too often too similar to the labruscas of Ontario to greatly change the taste of the resultant wine.

With the war's end, between 20 and 30 vines were nursed across the Atlantic from Europe; it was the beginning of care which would be the envy of the pediatrician. A vine removed from its homeland is as vulnerable as a child remote from its mother. The results cannot be known conclusively for five years, frequently longer. It may not like its new soil, it may not stand frost, it may be killed in January or surviving this, succumb in May. It may be subject to variants of mildew, or phylloxera, or any one of scores of other usually terminal afflictions. The weaning of those original European vines was practically parental-like but only four or five survived — and only two or three produced grapes sufficiently abundant to pass into the bottle. This might seem like defeat. To plant breeders and wine men it is an enormous success.

Other vines were brought across the water, from California and from New York. Some came from the famous Bordeaux area of southwest France — all were flops. Others came from Alsace and from Germany. They were not only average varieties of vines; half a dozen were among the best in the world. They were planted, fertilized, pruned, protected. The grapes from them were in some cases literally counted one by one, inspected, their juices analysed. Viticulture was becoming increasingly scientific not only in Canada but throughout the world. It all took a very long time but looking back to men like de Chaunac, it must have been worth every minute of endeavor. Canada today doesn't grow grapes of that class prolifically, but those top varieties, the Pinot Chardonnay and Pinot Noir for example, now grow in sufficient quantities to be an influential constituent in Canadian champagnes and white burgundy wines.

While de Chaunac and a few others were trying to make the European species adapt to Canadian ways, others – and again especially the plant breeders at Vineland station – were concentrating on hybridization, the art of crossing two different grape varieties to produce a third. In the past 25 years there have been on the average 100 different grape varieties under test on Vineland's 35-acre experimental plots beside the Queen Elizabeth Highway each year.

There is an adage in the grape breeding business – "the first acre is the hardest to obtain." How true this is may be judged by the grape called Vintage, which was bred by the plant scientists at Vineland's experimental farm. Like all the other thousands of cross-bred varieties tried out there, it started with a number. The first seeds were planted in 1949; only in 1967 was it considered to have prospered well enough to be given a name. That was a short time span for grape culture; it often takes 30 years to reach this stage, and even in this period it is likely that not a full acre of the new grapes will have been harvested.

The normal process at Vineland is for the cross-bred seed to be first planted in greenhouses. Often

175 seeds will be planted to get one hybrid vine; this takes two or three years. The vine is then planted outside. If it survives frost, bacteria and all the other menacing threats of nature, it will grow grapes that can be picked within three years. But a handful of any one variety is not enough. There must be sufficient vines to pick 11 quarts of grapes before any wine tests are made in the laboratories. If the wine is acceptable to the tasters at Vineland, vines of the variety may be sent out to a dozen growers in the Niagara Peninsula to be developed in different types of soils. Meanwhile, similar test plot experiments continue at Vineland. Some years after the 11-quart test (and this means eight to twelve years after the first cross-bred seeds were planted) the grapes are again made into wine and tested for clarity, colour, bouquet, flavour, and many other qualities at the station. Then samples of the wine are sent out in four-ounce bottles to commercial wineries, where it is again tested in laboratories and tasted. If the reaction is good, preparations are made to put the wine into commercial production or use it for blending with other grape juices. Further plantings will be made and more tests in subsequent years will be carried out. So the vines are developed, with checking year by year along the way. The wine may have the honour of receiving a name rather than a number and ultimately, when there are thousands of such vines, they may be offered to the nurseries for sale, may be bought and planted by the growers, and find their way each autumn into the crushing mills of the wineries.

Only people sure in their own knowledge who possess infinite patience, have the desire to create better products, and have unbounded faith in Canada, would have dared chart such long journeys. But it has been done. French hybrid grapes such as the many different Seibels are distinctive ingredients in Canadian wines today. Now the old Concord grape, which once accounted for 90% of all production in Canada, is down to 40%. New varieties have been grown; new tastes introduced. The wines of 1970 are greatly different from those of the early 1930's.

It is not only the grapes that have been changed. Back when a plethora of wineries opened in Ontario's grocery stores and when not too discriminating customers only demanded that the product appeared in something resembling a bottle bearing a wine label, the grapes were allowed to ferment through the action of the natural yeasts. It was a time when "you can't improve upon nature" was still the fallacious maxim of many of the profiteers as well as many of the lazy.

In the reconstruction era of the thirties, the better winemakers realized they could no longer be at the mercy of such a variable. The whims of the natural yeasts could provide a guffaw or a curse, but the wine companies were becoming bigger and wiser. So they and Vineland have experimented over the years, compared scientific notes with wine research stations in California and New York and Europe, noted the discoveries in the brewing and distilling industries throughout the world, and come up with their own carefully controlled yeasts.

Fickleness became a thing of the past. Now when the carefully weighed yeast is added, the winemaker knows what the reaction will be, precisely. Of course there were many obstacles to be overcome in this field too. One winemaker who experimented with yeasts for sherries over a long period has confessed that he was nonplussed because the yeasts wouldn't grow in the barrel as in Spain. One season he would find that they did, the next they didn't. The answer was temperature; just a degree or two difference meant success or failure. Now different yeast cultures are produced, stored in refrigerators, and used for champagnes, cheaper ports, dearer table wines. Some were brought from South Africa and altered; others were born in Andalusia and modified.

While the creation of new grape varieties and the development of yeasts have been the major changes affecting Canadian wines, there have been many more. In the field, new methods of pruning, trellising and setting out vines have been introduced. Grape growers have been taught the importance of fertilizing and anti-pest spraying. Smudge pots and wind-stirring helicopters have been tried in the battle against late spring frosts. Prices have been set to encourage the growing of vinifera or French hybrid grapes.

In the actual winemaking, the differences from the "bad old days" are even more noticeable. Most wineries now look more spick and span than dairies. While there are still, in a few instances, wooden casks 100 years old, wood is increasingly being replaced by stainless steel or epoxy-lined tanks. Diatomaceus earth is imported to filter the wine of its sediments. Sugar is stored in cool, hygienic quarters. There may be over 100 stages to bottling, including the one where any remaining bacteria in the empty bottles is destroyed.

There is inspection at all stages. Officials enforcing the Food and Drug Act of Canada, winery inspectors from the liquor boards of various provinces, health inspectors from municipalities, can pounce — and do. The control doesn't end when several hundred cases of wine leave the winery on a truck, but extends into the wine and liquor stores selling the product. A customer's complaint can mean several samples of a wine being taken, opened, analysed.

It all means that the Canadian can have the greatest confidence in his wine. And when it comes to taste, he is sure of a match for any in the world except those of the chateau-bottled vintage elite, which are the delight of the true connoisseur but are usually within reach of only the very rich.

CHAPTER SIX

The Latecomers

LOGANBERRIES grow well in only three areas of the world: Tasmania, the Franz Hoekeh valley in South Africa, and a region which includes the Pacific Northwest states of the U.S.A. and Canada's Vancouver Island. They do not like "wet feet" so they prefer growing conditions where the atmosphere is temperate, humid, and dew-like, rather than one with torrential rains.

On Vancouver Island, and notably on the Saanich Peninsula at the southern end, which claims to grow the best loganberries in the world, conditions are ideal. The rainfall in Victoria, at the base of this peninsula, is half that of Vancouver and less than in the states of Washington and Oregon. The Pacific breezes provide a funnelling effect which draws the rain away from the island towards the mainland leaving it with just the right amount of moisture and a year-round mild climate for the not too hardy loganberry. So loganberries have thrived on Vancouver Island. Unfortunately, there has never been a large population there. It was smaller 50 years ago when each year loganberries would rot in the fields for lack of buyers.

The loganberry growers decided to do something about this annual waste, and so it was that in 1921 a group of them formed a company to make loganberry wine. Thus was born, a century after Schiller had made wine in Ontario, the western half of Canada's wine industry.

For many years the only Canadian wine sold in British Columbia was this loganberry wine made by a company in Victoria. It is an origin which explains the paradox of Growers' Wine Company, the oldest and one of the biggest of today's wine companies outside Ontario. Basically, it is now a producer of grape wines, like all the others, but there it sits in the capital of British Columbia, on an island, and all its grapes have to be trucked hundreds of miles from either California or the interior Okanagan Valley and then cross the water to the plant.

In 1927, Herbert Anscomb, later a treasurer of British Columbia, was managing the Growers' Company. He decided it should enter the grape wine industry and made his first long-term contracts with Jesse Willard Hughes, whom we have already encountered tilling his soil in the Okanagan. Dr. Eugene Rittich, one of the several Hungarians who have contributed to the nation's wines, became the company's winemaker. Rittich was an old country idealist. He brought over vinifera vines from Europe and planted them in the Okanagan. Against all odds they grew, but each winter he had to completely bury the vines under soil because of the heavy frosts. Such labour costs never brought a profit, only satisfaction. The British Columbia industry had to survive on less exotic viticulture.

While the Growers' Wine Company was making loganberry wine and making its first ventures into grapes, Pasquale Capozzi was running a small store, the second grocery store to be started in Kelowna. He had arrived from Italy in 1906 with not even the proverbial shining dollar to be multiplied a million times in his pocket. But he did get more than a dollar for his first day's work; the Canadian Pacific Railway paid $1.25 a day to a section hand in that year. Capozzi wasn't a section hand for long. He worked as a sawmill operator, a lumberjack, and in a Revelstoke store. He found by travelling up and down the railway lines he could obtain a lot of grocery orders from the section hands. In 1913, he became the manager of the Consolidated Mining company store at the booming mining town of Trail. Three years later, he set up his own store in rough-and-tumble Phoenix in the British Columbia interior, which then had a population of 3,000, and 17 bars to quench its thirst.

Another three years later the mine closed down, dooming Phoenix to become a ghost town. Capozzi didn't wait to see it. From his savings he had bought a car, and the year after the First World War ended he started his own market survey by driving around the rough roads sketched between the mountains of British Columbia looking for a suitable place to open another grocery store.

On the outskirts of Kelowna, beside Lake Okanagan, a small boy was selling tomatoes in empty oil cans at the roadside. Capozzi stopped to buy some, and found they were selling at an unbelievable 25 cents per can. He asked the boy to check the price with his father, and indeed found it was correct. That clinched the deal and ended the survey as far as Capozzi was concerned. Any place, as he many times explained, that could produce tomatoes in such abundance must be an agricultural paradise. Capozzi had found the place for his grocery store. It was in the back of this store that what was to become British Columbia's largest winery was formed.

Pasquale Capozzi had taken a wife, Maria Anna. It is no exaggeration to credit her with the formation of the company, for in 1931, a new immigrant from Italy, Joseph Ghezzi, had dropped into the store. He was down and out, but so were most of the fruit farmers of the Okanagan Valley. No one was buying apples; they were rotting on the trees. Ghezzi had an idea how this circumstance of the Depression could be overcome – the apples should be picked and converted into apple wine. Maria Anna told her husband that something should be done to help Ghezzi and the farmers, many of whom were his grocery store customers. Capozzi listened, then talked to a few other small businessmen who agreed to meet Capozzi in the back of his store after business was over. They came, discussed the plan, and managed to scrape together $1,500 to form a company, which was named Domestic Wines and By-Products Ltd. One of the by-products was to be apple butter. A young Kelowna hardware merchant who was a teetotaller became the first president, his name was W.A.C. Bennett. He was later to become premier of British Columbia. Pasquale 'Cap' Capozzi was the vice-president.

The wine company never made any appreciable amount of either apple wine or apple butter in the thirties. In 1934, it changed its name to Calona Wines Ltd. and concentrated on making grape wines, but it was a small operation. Capozzi was mainly concerned with his groceries, Bennett with his nails and screws. War came, and British Columbia apples were in demand. The post-war period saw Bennett enter politics, become the first Social Credit premier of the province, and resign from the company. Calona Wines was a name unknown to all but a few Canadians, however, it did provide a training ground.

Pasquale Capozzi had had three sons – all interested in sports, all attended university, and all trained in the grocery store and the wine business. Herb Capozzi played professional football, entered politics, and became general manager of the British Columbia Lions football team. The other two, Joe and Tom, both ardent skiers, both university graduates, stayed with the wine company which by 1960 had passed almost completely into the control of the family.

At that time it was capable of making 400,000 gallons of wine. By the introduction of new methods, equipment, marketing, packaging, and general zest, the capacity in less than a decade rose to seven times that figure. Today Calona Wines furnishes 40% of the wine sold in British Columbia.

During the sixties, four other wineries were started in British Columbia and two others in Calgary and Moose Jaw to meet the growing Canadian taste for wine in the western half of the country. It is a different taste than that in the metropolises of

Toronto and Montreal, although this is rapidly changing.

The case of the fishing and hunting guide on a distant northern Manitoba lake can be taken as a rare exception. On a particularly cold snowy Thanksgiving Day weekend, a party of Winnipeg fishermen and their guide sat in a boat through the day. The guide spoke little but when he did it was in a cultured English university accent. They returned frozen to the guide's cabin that night where he lit a roaring fire and started to cook the few fish. It was at this stage that one of the party who appreciated the finer things of life produced a couple of bottles of fine wine from his pack. The guide disappeared and he was gone a considerable time. He returned wearing a somewhat creased, mildewed evening suit, black tie and white shirt. It must have been an apparition to those fishermen in their checkered shirts and thick trousers. The guide was quick to explain the transformation, "Never," he said, had he "worn evening dress since immigrating to northern Manitoba from Britain 30 years earlier for health reasons. But then never had anyone brought fine wine to his cabin before, and fine wine deserved the proper clothes."

Most people in the frontier land of the north are still more likely to do their wine drinking at the kitchen table. It is likely to come from a gallon jug, and possibly will be a berry wine.

The British Columbia wineries today continue to package wine in gallon bottles with a handle. It sells particularly well across the northern portions of the four western provinces. Calona Wines, though it was never successful with apple wines in its infancy, now makes large batches of it, and Growers' Wine still produces wines from loganberries, strawberries and other berries. They are all favorites of prairie farmers and miners' wives in small British Columbia towns.

Canadian wines, especially those of British Columbia are a product for the people. It is a point that may bore through re-emphasis, but so are the wines of any other country. The grand crus of France may be produced with a loving flourish by the sommeliers for the distinguished few, but for every such occasion there are a million times when vin ordinaire is swallowed in a farmer's field with cheese and bread, at checker-clothed tables in students' cafes, at stand-up bars, in the ordinary homes of very ordinary suburbs.

In British Columbia, the contrasts may not be so great, but they are there. Vancouver dockers call liebfraumilch "live frog's milk," and 300 miles away the latest winery, Mission Hill, stands above the Okanagan like a modern monastery, architecturally enviable by any of the great wine houses of Europe.

There are also marked basic conditions which affect winemaking in British Columbia. The art of winemaking is much younger on the West Coast; there hasn't been time for the experimentation with grape breeding and other factors which have now been part of the Ontario experience for a couple of generations. While better class hybrid grapes have in recent years been introduced in considerable quantities, they have been imported from the test plots of Ontario, New York, and other experimental areas of the continent.

Climate is greatly different. The vines of the Okanagan valley have to be hardier because winter temperatures can go lower. "Winter kill" is an ever-present consideration, particularly in the past decade there has been a higher-than-average incidence of death-dealing frosts in midwinter. The 200 grape growers of British Columbia must always be aware of this danger. Not surprisingly, they are unready to experiment with vines that have not been well tried under extreme conditions.

These growers used to be ruled by the dictum that if "you can see the lake (in Okanagan) and plant below 1,800 feet elevation" the grape will survive, but there are many who must have ignored the saying as vineyard acreage has jumped from 300 to nearly 3,000 in the past few years.

As long ago as 1899, a leading British Columbia botanist, G.W. Henry, planted 300 vines which were so successful that he was able to sit back and philosophise, "Let every person plant one vine at least next their door, and let them remember as they press the earth around its roots, and give it a final touch that they have not only provided a lasting pleasure for their own household, but they are handing down a source of health and happiness to the inmates of their home perhaps for generations to come." It is unlikely, though, that G.W. Henry saw the Okanagan from whence have sprung the modern vineyards. It has taken a lot more than a mere "pressing around the roots" there because this valley, and several of its spurs in the interior of British Columbia, is a geological freak. Originally, it was a near-desert on both sides of a narrow lake hemmed in by mountains, the tops of which have some of the heaviest precipitation in the world. As a measure of these desert conditions, even after the desert had been made to bloom, it is worth noting that at least one grower used to offer a "bounty" of two bottles of wine to anyone who caught a rattle-snake in his vineyard.

The heavy snows on the mountainside do reach the lake, but the slopes around it often only receive 12 inches of rainfall a year, and only a small part of this during the five-and-a-half month, frost-free, growing period. This means that the water from lake and river has to be pumped up and sprayed over every Okanagan vineyard. This irrigation coupled with the long hours of summer heat, results in heavy yields so that eight to ten tons of grapes per acre are not unknown – double the Ontario average. Yet the need for irrigation is a deterrent to the would-be grape grower. If it were simply a case of buying the 500 vines at 25 cents each and pressing them in the soil, there undoubtedly would be thousands in the business. But this is a minor cost factor when the acre of land may first cost $1,000 or more to acquire, and when another $500 has to be allowed per acre for irrigation equipment.

Yet interesting attempts to extend the grape lands are being made. One of these, near the town of Oliver, involves the use of Indian treaty lands for the first time in Canada. The Andres Wine Company, with the cooperation of the federal Department of Indian Affairs, has put in a Dutch-born supervisor to help the Indians become successful grape growers. If successful, it won't have been an easy victory, as the land has to be plowed, several cover crops grown and plowed in, irrigation systems constructed so the soil can be well watered – all before any vines are set out. But if this trial is a success, it could lead to extensive use of other Indian land. It could be a revolutionary turning point for the Indians.

Other areas of British Columbia might also become vineyard centres in the future. Henry suggested in the last century that the lower mainland around New Westminster would be ideal. Grapes do mature in the Fraser Valley and on the east coast of Vancouver Island but not readily enough for large commercial wineries. So it is more likely that apart from the use of more land near Oliver, new vineyards will be set out in the Lytton and Keremos regions of the interior where there are good sources of water for irrigation and where the summer heat ensures quick ripening.

The broader acreage is certainly needed. In Ontario, all wines have to be made from grapes produced in the province. This would be an impossibility in British Columbia at the present time. Thus, while the Ontario growers have 8,000 to 10,000 tons of grapes left over each year which they export to the U.S. wineries, the wineries in British Columbia regularly import 10,000 tons of grapes from California. Officially, the British Columbia government has a quota of U.S. grapes which can be imported but it isn't imposed very stringently for the simple reason that the growers of the province, and particularly in a year of frost, can't come anywhere near approaching the growing needs of the winemakers.

As a matter of interest, if every Canadian who now buys a bottle of wine convinced a friend to do the same, the whole industry would be in turmoil; it simply couldn't cope. It would mean that the Ontario grape surplus would immediately disappear, and probably grapes would have to be imported after a change of legislation. In British Columbia, the situation would be even worse because, under present circumstances, the Thompson Seedless grape from the San Joaquin Valley of California is the base for British Columbia wine.

The hundreds of tons of these grapes, barreling northward in refrigerated trucks each year, and arriving as fresh as if they were picked on a neighboring hillside, has meant a much higher degree of hybrid vine growing in the British Columbia interior than in Ontario. So the various Seibels, the Himrods, the Rieslings are grown in considerable quantities to add their distinctively flavored juices to the wines of this province.

Only about 40 of the 200 grape growers have more than 20 acres to plant with these hybrids – an indication of how young the craft is when measured in old world terms. This means that usually a man has such close contact with his vines that they are practically part of his family. Perhaps this is why one wife said of her husband when he produced eight tons to the acre, "of course he kissed each grape good morning and good night." The folksiness of this statement can be multiplied throughout the Okanagan valley, an area of pleasant summer resort towns and tiny villages. Everybody seems to know that a certain hybrid which was tried became the favorite diet of the local pheasants, and that the Rieslings which are now successful were brought into the valley by some immigrants about 30 years ago and that they produce a wine which tastes quite different than German Rieslings. Only an industry that is very young and still comparatively small would find the time to remember such things. It won't always be that way.

Penticton has a motel unit for every ten inhabitants. It had 6,600 delegates to one convention in 1969. It talks of 20-storey apartment blocks which

78

are bound to rise. It has its small winery, Casabello Wines, which is aiming for higher quality wines.

Northward, at Kelowna, the Calona Wines has as its president, Pasquale Capozzi, one-time section hand who was recently given a doctorate of Notre Dame University. Calona produces apple wine with an alcoholic content nearly as high as the fortified wines of Canada, and has introduced decanters as containers for all its wines.

Down at the meetings of fresh and salt water, in the environs of Vancouver and Port Moody and New Westminster, Andres Wines and Villa Wines have opened plants to meet the growing taste of British Columbians for wine. And over in the old loganberry wine plant of Victoria there is a vast range of wines being produced.

British Columbia is one the newest places in the world to make wine, and what has happened there can only be called a beginning, but a fast one.

CHAPTER SEVEN

Wine Is
As Complex As Man

THE first-time visitor to a winery is invariably
disappointed. In his quick tour, if it be an old style
plant in Europe, he will pass through rows of wood-
en vats black with age and so high that he can't look
over the top to see what is inside. In Canada, he
would best remember all the stainless steel, the
valves, the hoses on the floor. At the finish, he gets
a sample – but not in Canada, where it is illegal –
and then leaves the smell of wine, which is common
to every winery, with but a single thought, "Where
are those people who trample on the grapes?" They
are not there, probably have never been there, because, as has been pungently said, man is the mid-
wife of newborn wine so he certainly wouldn't
trample on his product. The myth of a bunch of
peasants, their ankles purple with juice, performing
some frenzied pagan dance couldn't be further from
the truth of a Canadian winery at vintage time, for
then it is as organized, as sterile, as hectic as any
maternity ward.

Out of those first grapes, and succeeding hundreds of tons of grapes arriving each autumn at the wineries of Ontario will be born wine. Nobody knows precisely how it will turn out, whether it will have personality and be accepted by society or will be rejected. Nobody knows how its character will develop. Nobody knows exactly how long it will live. Nobody knows when it will reach the zenith of its career. It is like man.

It may, though this is still unlikely in Canada, age a hundred years like some of the Madeira wines and still be at the peak of palatability.

It may, and this is now even more unlikely, be so poorly treated in its weaning period, by too much heat or too much cold in the incubation of the fermenting tank that it may fade and die before 12 months are past.

It will usually reach perfection much earlier if it is a white table wine than if it is a sherry.

It will be reared a lot differently, according to whether it is a red, white or rosé wine and will be strengthened if it is intended to live a longer life as a dessert wine.

It will be given "beauty treatments" to make it clear and attractive.

The germs around it will be destroyed and chemicals will be added to it, almost like medicines, and in the end, when the last drop is drunk, it is hoped that its life will have been a worthwhile endeavor, like any man's.

If the similarity to man seems preposterous, then listen to Ted Phillips, the man responsible for production at the Parkdale Wine Company. He thinks it should be extended to the grapes themselves. It has already been noted that the basic grape species common to Canada is the vitis labrusca, and that the basic grape species in Europe is the vitis vinifera. Mr. Phillips asks, "Who is to say which is the best?" And answers, "Only time will tell."

If the vision of grape trampling can be so easily dispensed with, the epitome of the winemaker who is the wine lover still is personified in this man who grows vines successfully in his suburban Toronto garden besides bringing into being improved Canadian wines as his daily craft. Mr. Phillips also thinks about wine, "Children should be the wine tasters; a child's taste is the keenest. As we grow older, our taste buds deteriorate and actually fatigue. Look at an older person eating spaghetti; he tastes the first few mouthfuls and bolts the rest. The Europeans take longer over their meals because the wine they take with them not only cleans the palate but reactivates the tastes, so the food is better appreciated on at least two counts."

The juice of the grape, then, is the child from which the wine is born. Without extending the parallel to man further, it should be pointed out that each grape is also 80% water.

A hint has already been given that it is the remaining 20% which distinguishes the grape from other fruits, and makes it the best for the making of wine. There is a high degree of sugar present in the form of dextrose and levulose; there are tartaric, malic, citric, phosphoric, oxalic and another score of different acids; there are tannins, enzymes, vitamins, a dozen or more minerals, proteins, and a dozen different pigment agents. To this array is added yeast, and the enormously complicated process of fermentation takes place.

It wasn't until the last century that any major

attempt was made to find out how the fermentation process works. About the time the first Canadian vineyards were being planted, Louis Pasteur began his studies of wine which were to change him from a renowned chemist into the world's leading microbiologist. Between 1860 and 1862, he observed that whenever fermentation took place a living germ – which multiplied – could be detected. He had already found out that the air contained microorganisms ready to multiply and had even climbed part way up Mont Blanc to show there were less microbes in the purer air at higher altitudes.

Pasteur, whose work has probably saved millions of lives, worked frequently in a wine cafe, rather than a dairy, near his father's house in the small town of Arbois in the foothills of the Jura mountains. He saw customers drinking the wine every day, and soon was to discover that the wild yeasts on the grapes from which it had been made were deposited there from the air with the dust. This was but the first step in the introduction of unhygienic parasites to the wine. Others were brought to the vats by the workers, and the grape presses were often unclean. All of these factors brought diseases during bottle fermentation. Pasteur then made his great step forward. He heated wines to 130 degrees Fahrenheit, and held them at that temperature for several minutes. The wine was cooled, and kept thereafter in airtight containers. Pasteurization had been invented.

However, would the taste of the wine be destroyed? A commission of leading wine tasters met on Nov. 23, 1865 to find out. They sampled 21 wines of different vintage. The differences between the heated and unheated wines were so minute that they escaped nine out of ten of the experts. By the time, two years later, when Canada's Clair House Vineyards were finding renown in Europe, the French wine industry had totally accepted pasteurization.

What Pasteur did then is still an integral part of winemaking even though many other processes have been introduced to present a completely hygienic product. Germ-free cleanliness is as vital to wine as it is to the child.

Perhaps it is time that we looked at the rearing of this child, which is wine. As with the rearing of children, there are certain common denominators. There is a whole body of intelligence which is shared throughout the world on the best methods to be followed. But just as the Spanish muchacho is brought up slightly differently from the Italian bambino or the French enfant or the Canadian pre-school age youngster, so there are differences between Spanish, Italian, French and Canadian winemaking practices. In addition, just as the parent in Victoria may have a few different ideas to one in St. Catharines, and even the one in St. Catharines from the one in Niagara Falls, so there are some differences in winemaking within a single country.

Now we present the basic form of wine-making in Canada. The first important step is to get the grapes from the vineyards to the winemaking plant quickly to avoid any despoilation after they are picked. The grapes themselves must be at their peak, with the right degree of sugar content and acidity. This can only be achieved given the right weather, and includes sufficient hot, sunny days and the right amount of moisture. A complication in

Ontario is that because different varieties of grapes achieve their optimum for winemaking purposes in different lengths of time, some are ready for picking in early September while others can't be harvested until mid-October. And grapes in October can be subject to frost.

The growers bring their grapes to the winery for weighing and testing for sugar content. They are then put through a crusher, which smashes the skins without smashing the seeds and removes the stems. It is at this stage that there is an immediate parting of the ways, according to whether white or red wine is to be made. If it is white wine, the grape pulp and juice pass into a press after separation from the skins and seeds, the pulp undergoes pressure, and the juice is squeezed out. For a red wine, pulp, juice, skins and seeds pass onto the fermentation tank. The skins provide the red colour of this wine through their natural pigmentations; the seeds provide tannin which is often required to provide the sharp, distinctive taste of most red wines. The rosé (pink) wine is half-way in colour between a red and a white wine so that to make this wine, juice, pulp, skins and seeds are only allowed to remain in the fermentation tank for a short time, usually not more than a day, to impart just the right degree of colour before seeds and skins are removed.

The mixture that goes to the fermentation tanks is called the "must." The tanks holding it may be of wood, stainless steel, glass-lined, or concrete, and have capacities up to hundreds of thousands of gallons.

Immediately the must is treated with sulphur dioxide in liquefied form or a sulphurous salt to kill the natural yeasts and other parasites of the grape, and reduce oxidation, and help clarify the wine. Only a miniscule quantity of sulphur dioxide is necessary for this purpose, and its addition must be carefully controlled; too much and the wine would be ruined. At the same time, sugar and the carefully prepared yeast cultures are added.

If this all sounds like tinkering with nature, and in the case of sulphur dioxide positively noxious, it should be again reiterated that these scientific additives are now common to winemaking throughout the world.

The fermentation tank temperature must be carefully controlled, as grape must is highly volatile. A batch of fermenting grapes has been known to bend an iron bar, and, as has been noted earlier, in extremely hot weather a fermenting tank can go out of control. This is now unknown because of the cooling systems that have been introduced to siphon off the heat produced in the tanks, which now never goes above 85 degrees Fahrenheit for red table wines nor above 60 degrees for white wines. These controlled temperatures bring a slow, regular fermentation responsible for a higher yield of alcohol, less infection from bacteria, and a wine that is clearer and with a better aroma.

Already there has been an important difference in procedure according to whether the wine to be made is red or white or rosé. There is another procedure according to whether it will be a table wine or a dessert wine. The table wines are the light wines usually taken with meals that have an alcoholic content of not more than 14%. The dessert wines, sometimes called aperitifs, have a higher alcoholic content – sometimes 20%. They include sherries, ports, muscatels, vermouths. To achieve this higher alcoholic content, brandy made at a distillery is added to the must. In the case of better ports, the spirit is added early and the wine is put away in casks to age. With sherries, the spirit is normally added after aging and just before bottling. These additions are carefully checked in Canada by the customs and excise branch. Adding the alcohol naturally increases the alcoholic content of the wine but it also stops the action of the yeast so that some of the sugar in the must is unconverted to alcohol. The effect is to give a sweeter tasting wine. The point at which the alcohol is added therefore depends on the degree of sweetness which is wanted in the final product. Generally, alcohol is added earlier for ports than for sherries because a sweeter taste is required of the former.

With a red table wine, the must is checked for colouration. When this is considered right for the final product, the skins and pulp are removed from the juice, which as this stage is called "the free run." The removed pulp is then passed through a wine press where the juice is forced out. This juice returns with the "free run" juice to complete its slow fermentation.

At the end of this process there can be once again a different procedure if a sparkling wine such as Champagne is going to be made. These are made from table wines, but have to go through a secondary fermentation in closed tanks. Sugar and pure yeast cultures are added. The first fermentation of grape must has produced a great quantity of carbon dioxide, which is unused; a secondary fermentation produced more, which cannot escape. This creates an internal pressure of five atmospheres (one atmosphere equals 15 pounds pressure per square inch) in the bottle of sparkling wine. It is this pressure that accounts for the pop when a bottle is opened, the bubbles and the fizz when the wine is poured.

Grape juice for a white or red table wine moves from the tanks where it has been fermenting to equally huge vats for settling. Here suspended yeast cells and small particles of skin or pulp soon find their own level – at the bottom of the tank. The wine is still active, and chemical processes continue causing some minor fermentation. It is here, most particularly, that the subtleties of individual wines are made by the actions of the tiny residual chemicals upon each other.

The next important stage is "racking" and "fining." The wine is racked off, being taken from its settling tank and thus being separated from its lees – the word used to describe the sludge of pulp and yeast particles. This process is repeated many times, especially for the better class of wines.

Racking alone is not sufficient to clear the wine to the standards required by today's drinkers. So fining substances, which screen out minute particles in the wine, are introduced. Favorite fining materials have been isinglass and the whites of eggs. In fact, a legend of Spain, but no more than a legend, is that chickens were bred which produced eggs with extra large whites for the fining of that country's sherries. In Canada, as in many other parts of the world, diatomaceous earth and bentonite clay is found more practical, and, as elsewhere, a lot of fining is now accomplished by filtration under pressure or a rapid sequence of heating and chilling.

At this juncture, the grape has been turned into

wine. It is clear, clean, fairly robust, colourful. It can stand on its own feet. It is the least costly wine in North America, comparable to the vin ordinaire or vino de casa of Europe.

To develop character to be remembered, to take on a delightful aroma an even more delightful taste, it has to be aged.

This is as complex as the original steps of winemaking. The wine historically was always aged in wooden, usually oak, casks. Now it is being done in huge tanks, too. No one knows every single thing that happens to wine as it ages, but we do know that there is continued oxidation, the esters go on doing their work, but there are still, although man has now stepped onto the moon, riddles in this field. What is known adds up to greatness in a wine for the drinker. The new wine, through age, loses its harshness, drops in acidity, and comes forth as a delicate beverage. The red wine becomes more ruby-like in colour; the white wine turns golden. Aging is the most crucial of the vintner's tasks. If he takes a wine from the cask and puts it into bottles too early he may destroy it, or at least reduce its fine qualities. If he does it too late the results may be equally disastrous.

There are certain rules, of course. Table wines, particularly whites, and sparkling wines, age quickly. If the wine snob boasts of a wine of these categories over ten years old, you will know he knows nothing about wine. Dessert wines age slowly; as a general rule the more years a sherry or port have aged the better they will be. But even within the framework of these rules, it is a tricky business.

After aging, the wine is bottled. This is now done on high speed bottling lines where each bottle is cleaned, inspected, filled, capped, labelled, and passed to the packing case within minutes. The bottle of wine then proceeds by truck or rail to wine stores and liquor stores in Canada where it is kept under controlled temperature because even at this stage excess heat or cold can mitigate its qualities.

Aging goes on in the bottle, as well as in the original cask, for wine is a living thing – alive until the moment you drink it. The main tenet of the winemaker who produces this living thing is to keep a check on nature, for nature will complete a cycle, changing the sugar in the grape to wine and then to vinegar and then to water. The oenologist has to hold the wine from passing on to the next stage while at the same time improving it. He has some advantages in Canada. The high acidic content of most of the grapes which are used provides a "clean" fermentation. It isn't necessary, for example, as it is in Spain to add gypsum to make up for low acidity.

However, despite these repeated references to chemicals, it cannot be emphasized too strongly that the human element remains an overriding factor in the making of wine. The winemaker must have scientific knowledge, a high standard of ethics, long experience, an inborn awareness of dangers, a feeling for grapes, a love of wine. He must know that the yeast cell is just alive but inactive in the fermentation tank if the temperature is down to 34 degrees, that it is active at 60 degrees, and can die if the thermometer reaches the high nineties. Equally, he must know that poor wine will result if poor grapes are delivered at the crusher, that there will be too great a tannin taste if the stalks are left on too long, that a poor cask can give a woody flavor, that the wine will be too acid if the grapes aren't fully ripe, that the addition of too much sugar will mean a dull, neutral taste, that extra sugar in one fermentation can produce bouquet at the cost of "body," and in another fermentation exactly the reverse. And a thousand other things. His problems are multiplied in Canadian wineries because, unlike those elsewhere, every individual winery makes such a wide variety of wine products. Each one also blends its wines so that just one of its products may be made from a collection of different grape juices. This complicates procedures enormously.

It is time to visit these individual wineries of Canada to see how they differ as parents to their wines.

CHAPTER EIGHT

The
Canadian Wineries

BLOOD is the best fining agent for the clarification of wine. It is used legitimately and exten-
sively throughout the world, but not in Canada
where its use is banned. Perhaps the wine drinker
will be appalled to learn that such a product might
have been used to clean his favorite imported drink
– he shouldn't be. Blood isn't used in Canada, but
bentonite clay is as are gases and acids in the making
of wine, just as they are used in processing many
foods that we use daily. It is all a matter of degree.
Both fluorine and chlorine are now added to the
water supplies of many Canadian cities, and hardly
anyone gives them a second thought because the
result of adding these chemicals is almost imper-
ceptible.

The additives in the making of wine are even
harder to notice. In fact, if they are noticed it will
be by those in the wine industry who taste the wine
first, and the wine will never reach the public. This
checking is never-ending, not only by various gov-

ernment agencies charged with the job but by individual wineries. One of these checks – it is almost a rite – takes place daily in the heart of Toronto. The Toronto Dominion Building rises 54 floors, the tallest building in the British Commonwealth. It is the quintessence of modern functionalism and the epitome of the Bauhaus influence on 20th-century architecture. It is the hub of the city's financial district, overshadowing the stock exchange. Express elevators bypass the lower 40 or so floors; a piece of scrap paper would never disgrace its corridors – it is clean, efficient, super-modern, a long way from the vineyard of classical-paintings or Biblical reference. In this building is located the head office of the Jordan Wine Company. There is not a whiff of grapes. Eskimo sculptures grace the coffee tables; abstracts adorn the walls. Guests sink into luxurious chesterfields. The typewriters are electric, the desks have been evenly spaced with a micrometer. There is not a label, a bottle, a cardboard carton in sight. It is clean, efficient, super-modern, a long way from the basement under a small apartment block on Toronto's Danforth Avenue, where this company (then known as the Danforth Wine Company) began in the 1920's.

There is, however, still a common tie to those early days. Then Fred Torno, who formed the company, tasted his product every day even though, because of health reasons, he has never been a heavy wine drinker. Today his sons, Philip and Noah, the principals of what has become one of Canada's largest wine corporate structures, sip the wine of their company each day at noon to check its quality. Samples of the latest batch of wine ready to be placed on the market are sent to them and there, high above the stockbrokers and typists hurrying out to lunch, the final test is made to ensure that Canadians are getting a good wine.

Such checkings proceed regularly in other wineries even if the surroundings may vary. The differences in detail apply throughout the winemaking industry even though the basic winemaking process outlined in the previous chapter is common to all. They necessitate a quick survey of some of the variations to be found in wineries located on the byways of southern Ontario, in the interior of British Columbia, and elsewhere across the land.

Barnes Wines, being the oldest, shall have pride of place. The city of St. Catharines is now pressing in on this ancient winery. But for the present, its own surrounding test plots of vineyards act as a moat although they may not do so forever. Urban growth, industrial expansion, highway building are the great enemies of present Canadian viticulture. The Queen Elizabeth Highway, built before 1939 as Canada's first freeway, used up thousands of acres of good vineyard land. The Great God Car is demanding even more room, and now the Q.E.W. is being widened and again consuming more vineyards.

The Barnes Winery is near all this activity. It is deceivingly small because most of its larger storage tanks are underground. However, outside – and this is a growing practise of all wineries – are a string of 50,000 gallon, glass-lined, metal tanks. For the mathematically inclined, each of these tanks holds 300,000 bottles of wine. The winery may appear small, but it does sell "western mickeys", gallon flagons of wine, on the prairies – as do other

Ontario producers, as well as those of British Columbia.

Barnes is also exceptional in being able to sell in every province of Canada; this is no mean accomplishment. The individual liquor boards decide which "listings" they will allow; this is determined by a number of factors, the most practical one being storage space, not only in their central, provincial warehouses but in each province's chain of liquor stores. Because of the tens of thousands of different makes of wines available from all parts of the world, the liquor boards have to select a small proportion only, otherwise their facilities would be overwhelmed. Most Canadian wineries produce 20 to 30 different brands each, and although Canadian wines get some preference in most parts of the country, there isn't storage space for all of these in some smaller provinces. Many of the Canadian wineries don't consider they are given sufficient preferential treatment, but it must be allowed that the liquor boards have to make difficult choices. They have to balance the consumer's taste for imported and domestic wines, sweet or dry, table or dessert before making an initial decision whether to grant a particular wine a "listing." Afterwards matters get easier; they can apply the yardstick of demand. If a particular wine does not sell well and takes up valuable storage space, the liquor board can decide that the wine shall be struck from its rolls.

Barnes hold the distinction of having at least one of its products available in every part of the country partly because of the age of the company. But it is an achievement which presents marketing problems since there are no uniform marketing regulations in Canada. One province demands specific wording on labels, another has its own ideas regarding bottles or caps or cartons. With ten masters to obey, all shipments have been stored separately, and this means costlier warehousing arrangements at the St. Catharines winery. It also means that not all Barnes products go through the bottling line at the winery. For instance, the Quebec liquor board buys Barnes wines in bulk and bottles them even though Barnes supplies the bottles, caps, and labels.

Barnes is exceptional in one other regard. There is a Barnes champagne although the winery doesn't make it. It buys the champagne from another, larger producer and bottles it under its own label to maintain a full range of wines.

The age of the company shows though in other than acquiring country-wide sales. It is reflected in some of its 80-year-old storage casks which are kept filled so that they will never dry out and shrink. This precious care is taken because oak is still the best wood for aging although it is now difficult to obtain and has been replaced by redwood, which is cheaper but requiries treatment with soda ash or sulphuric acid to draw out the resins. The redwood casks then have to be filled with cheap wine which is allowed to ferment before they can be brought into proper service in the production of saleable wine.

The removal of the tartrates in wine is essential to the stabilization of the product. At Barnes, the temperature of the wine is brought down to 19 degrees, and it is held at this level for three weeks before any other processing.

A few miles away, at Niagara Falls, is Brights,

the largest winery in Canada, using 20,000 tons of grapes a year, storing eight million gallons of wine, bottling 12,000 gallons a day. This all suggests modernity but there are still oak casks in use that were brought from Toronto in the 1890's.

Brights have repeatedly been the first in Canadian wine ventures. In 1934, a plant was opened in Lachine to bottle Brights wines for the province of Quebec. Twenty years later they added a champagne cellar specifically built at Niagara Falls so that the entire life cycle of the first bottle-fermented wine to be made in volume could be conducted under one roof. One of every three bottles of champagne bought by Canadians comes from this cellar. They have been pioneers in grape testing, having brought hundreds of varieties into the country for experimentation.

Winemaking is highly controlled; so is grape growing. Apart from caring for their own 1,000 acres, Brights field men act as advisors to individual growers who are suppliers – even the largest suppliers who may for years have sent 500 tons of grapes annually to this one winery. This advice includes telling the growers when to grow alfalfa or other enrichening crops between their vines, when to fertilize, when to spray, when to cultivate, when to pick. Precise records are kept to check when each stage is carried out in the vineyards.

The records multiply in the winery. There is now not only a company check; government officials do, too. An Ontario liquor board inspector watches the weighing of the grapes as they arrive at the winery, for in this way he can ensure that not more than the legal limit of 250 gallons of wine per ton of grapes is being made. This is a small token of their power, as these representatives of the liquor board can order the alteration of any equipment, the removal of any fruit, marc or pomace considered unsanitary from the premises, extend the aging of a wine, inspect all bottles, and much more. This isn't a power which has to be exercised at Brights, whose aim for years has been a better product. Nevertheless, a periodic inspection is made, for instance, when the wines are chilled down to 18 degrees Fahrenheit for a week to remove all tartrates before they are filtered, or a look is taken at the process whereby better class sherries in barrels are steam heated at 135 degrees for rapid aging.

And the customs and excise men are always on hand when alcohol is added to such fortified wines as sherries and ports. The alcohol may have originated from grapes which came into the Brights plant, and the alcohol is actually stored there. But it is padlocked, and cannot be opened without the presence of an excise man to check the precise quantity being added to any batch of wine.

At the other extreme to the government concern over use of the last ounce of alcohol is the sheer volume of wine produced by this company. One hundred and seventy bottles are received from cartons, sterilized, inspected, filled, capped, labelled and packaged again in cartons every minute. It would be impossible by man alone. Photo electric cells help him. They do all the counting so that the records are as complete for this last stage as for the first.

Niagara Falls not only has an abundance of tumbling water, it has a healthy supply of bottled wine. Not far from the Brights plant, Chateau Gai Wineries is representative of the Canadian mosaic. It started as the Stamford Park Wine Company in 1890, and again some of the original barrels are in use. But so are 4,000 white oak barrels brought from Kentucky, and each weighing 100 pounds. A regulation of that southern state was that the charred oak barrels could only be used once for aging Bourbon whisky. This suited Chateau Gai, for it meant that no initial wine fermentation was necessary before they were put to use. By the late 1920's, Canadian Wineries Ltd. had absorbed the original company and others in Oakville, Toronto, St. Catharines, Thorold. It was already selling sauternes and claret type table wines, and before the Second World War, it was selling wine, too, throughout the West Indies. The company by then had a new president, A. G. Sampson, and he liked the ring of one of the company's brand names, Chateau Gai. So in 1940, he changed the firm's name.

Today, the winemaker is Algerian, one assistant is German and another is English but speaks five languages. This latter talent isn't essential to winemaking but it helps; recently the Englishman was translating Russian documents on winemaking for the company.

The grapes from 250 growers come to this large winery each autumn. At one time, in the 1940's and 1950's, the wine made from this intake was stored in concrete tanks. Like other wineries, Chateau Gai found this was a costly "borrowing" of a European method. The tanks cracked and soon had to be abandoned. Now glass lined tanks holding more than a million gallons are used in the blended wine cellar. But this is only part of the 2,750,000 gallons at Chateau Gai's plant. All of this wine has to be moved from stage to stage by a system of stainless steel pumps and plastic hoses.

The old-fashioned home winemaker swore by a wooden spoon and an earthenware crock. "Never must grape juice touch metal," fathers earnestly warned their sons. Then came the 20th century, and throughout the world metal was being used in wineries.

Chateau-Gai wanted to make sure the old beliefs could be routed; that it was absolutely safe to use metals – and not only safe, for there could be no reduction in quality. So as long ago as 1934, when the company was still Canadian Wineries, a full study was launched with the International Nickel Company to find out the tolerance of wines for metals. More than 400 corrosion tests were conducted on seven different metals. Tin and iron were found unsuitable for winery use; most of the others, like copper and aluminium were useful in certain equipment; stainless steel was harmless and did not affect the colour, clarity or taste of wines stored in it. Much testing of metals in relation to wine has succeeded that set of experiments.

Thus at the Jordan Wines plant at St. Catharines, where the products (except champagne) which are tasted daily in the heart of Toronto are made, ion exchange is responsible for removing the cream of tartar (potassium bitartrates) from the wine. It is ironical that some Canadians don't object to the odd black fleck in a bottle of expensive imported wine, but immediately complain to their local liquor board if they see a single crystal marring the clarity of a Canadian product. And that is what the potassium bitartrates form. They are harmless but the customer won't accept them. So they are changed into sodium bitartrates and the wine is stabilized. It all used to be done by prolonged refrigeration, but many wineries now use the ion exchange method because it's cheaper and speedier. Both are factors in major wine production.

At Jordan's the crushers take 45 to 65 tons of grapes an hour. There are a series of three presses, the last of which exerts a pressure of 350 tons, so that the last droplet of grape juice can be obtained, and the must is pumped at the rate of 150 gallons a minute. One fermentation tank alone, possibly the world's largest, holds 100,000 gallons, and at the same time grape concentrate is stored in eight small tanks. This, when reconstituted, can make half a million gallons of wine.

So far the wineries we have visited have been on rural roads or only beginning to feel the thrust of urbanization from their situation at the edge of Niagara Peninsula towns. Parkdale Wines and the Turner Wine Company are far from the grape, both in Metropolitan Toronto. Yet both are different.

The Parkdale plant is beside the Queen Elizabeth Way in the western suburbs. The Turner company couldn't be more central, as it is in the original town of York from which Toronto grew. The Parkdale complex is low and sprawling, Turner's is in an upright stone building that could be the subject for a woodcut illustrating a Victorian novel.

Tens of thousands of Toronto workers from the suburbs know one thing about the Parkdale headquarters they pass each morning; it is the first to put up Christmas greetings in lights each year to welcome the commuter. They should recognize another fact about Parkdale from the hundreds of barrels pyramided in the grounds of the plant – its cooperage is bigger than for that of many Canadian wineries. These hundreds of barrels are not cleaned each time they are used because the wine that has aged in them adds qualities to the wood which benefits each successive wine.

Parkdale, like its competitors in the Niagara Peninsula, maintains test plots there and is always trying to get growers to take new varieties to replace the old vines. But each and every single grape used in its winemaking has to be shipped into Toronto from 60 to 80 miles away.

The base for the wines of its subsidiary, Normandie Wines of Moncton, New Brunswick, come even farther – from the vineyards of Europe. It is a radical departure. A few years ago, the Normandie company was formed to make blueberry wine. The blueberries are usually picked by Indians in the open, rocky areas between the forests of the maritime province. These Indians know where to find the best fruit – where the land has been recently burned over. An agent in turn buys the fruit for the company which produces a wine in the same way as if the fruit were grapes. And, in truth, without the label it would be hard to tell that the resulting product wasn't made from grapes because there is very little distinctive blueberry taste.

Blueberry wine is popular particularly in the Maritime provinces. However, Normandie soon found the capacity of its plant was being wasted with only blueberry wine, so it was decided to bring in concentrated grape juices from Europe for the making of other wines; these wines are now being sold across Canada. For ports and sherries, the wine juices are brought from Iberia; for white table wines, the juice comes from Germany; and for reds, juice is imported from France, Italy and Greece.

Just as Normandie's specialty is blueberry wine, a cherry wine is a best seller of the Turner company, and honey wines have become associated with the London Winery. Yet the practises used with these specialty wines remain approximately the same as when grapes are used; and, in London Winery, grape wines remain by far the bulk of production.

That is why at this plant outside the prosperous city of London there is storage space for a 1,000 tons of sugar.

As elsewhere, the fermentation tanks and the laboratory are the two keys to the total operation, and it is not surprising to find that plug-in telephones link the two. These are greatly in use when the 20,000 gallon B.C. fir tanks have been emptied for cleaning, preparatory to receiving new "must." Gas masks are now provided for workers on this job, unlike earlier times when, according to Charley McCarthy, who has been employed at London Winery for 30 years and is now its sales manager, a candle was provided to light the way. Now, too, ventilation fans go into the tanks when men are working inside them so that it is no longer necessary, in Mr. McCarthy's words, "to watch the candle, and when it went out, you got out." Even so, the plug-in phones, gas masks and fans still provide additional safety measures today.

We have noted different individual methods employed at various stages of fermentation – racking, storage, and bottling. This applies as much to the smaller wineries as the larger ones. The Beau Chatel winery beside the Queen Elizabeth Highway at Winona near Hamilton has a brand new building with many modern scientific means, such as spreading carbon dioxide in a mist over the grape crushing operation to prevent oxidation, but it falls back on rice hulls as an aid in pressing the pulp. These hulls open up the pumice to let the juice be extracted easier.

This winery, recently acquired by Andres Wines of British Columbia, also filters all water used in its winemaking to ameliorate any acids; stores any sugar to be added to its wines in liquid form in huge tanks; and "polishes" its wines by passing them through asbestos pads before bottling.

Abbey Wines, a comparatively new winery at Truro, Nova Scotia on the main road to Halifax, uses glass-lined storage tanks for the wines it makes of Californian grapes. Calona Wines in British Columbia does the same thing on a much bigger scale, but its red wines are stored in wood, a much more difficult product to clean after it has stored wine over a long period. All Calona's red wines are first passed through a centrifuge, not only to speed production but because it reduces the cleaning necessary for the inside of the wooden tanks.

Growers Wines Company in Victoria also uses a centrifuge for initial clarification of its wine, which is then stored in vats made of white oak brought from the Ozarks in the southern States. It ferments here before going on to its final clarification, where it is passed through pads with holes one-seventh the diameter of a yeast cell. No wonder Canadian wine in the bottle is so clear and free of impurities! Growers, like many other British Columbia wineries, does not add grape spirit to fortify its sherries and ports, but achieves a high alcoholic content through natural fermentative processes.

Andres Wines and Villa Wines both have their plants in greater Vancouver. Both use the same grade and variety of Californian grape, which may have been picked and shipped on the same day. But they have their subtleties of wine making that produce a difference in taste.

Casabello and Mission Hill may only be separated by half the length of Okanagan Lake and look to the vineyards sloping down to the lake for their main constitutent, but they aim for a difference in their wines – and so use slight differences in approach to their winemaking.

It is these differences that ensure for the customer such a wide range of products, and because most wineries only introduce them in search for a better quality product, the Canadian wine drinker is always the gainer. Winemaking in Canada may, generally, follow a basic universal pattern, but there are enough differences in equipment, treatments, and final tasting to guarantee that while Canadian wines may result from a blending of grapes rather than being made like vintage wines from one year's grapes from a single district, they are far from uniform when you drink them.

CHAPTER NINE

The Fortified Wines

THE world's commonly recognized fortified wines are sherry, port, muscatel, Madeira, vermouth, Malaga and Marsala. Of these, Madeira, Malaga and Marsala are nearly always made in their native areas of Europe and so need not be considered in reference to Canadian wines. Except that the author, who has a weakness for alliteration, would like to describe them all as magnificent, but so is sherry.

As the sales of Canadian sherry have always been and still are far greater than for any other variety of wine, the good taste of the Canadian drinker cannot be denied. Even such a relatively small Canadian winery as Chalet Wines located on the Trans Canada Highway between Calgary and Banff makes from its imported Californian grapes four different brands of sherry. It only offers 14 different brands of wine altogether.

The popularity of sherry is nothing new. Although it is generally thought to be a Spanish drink made specifically in the town of Jerez de la Frontera and fragments of wine jars with the markings "Jerez" were found in ancient Rome, something very close to the sherry we drink today was believed to have been consumed 2,000 years before the Roman Empire. Nevertheless, sherry and Spain are inseparable. In that country, sherry of a lower alcoholic content than that which is exported is used liberally as a table wine with every meal.

By the 14th century there was already a thriving Spanish sherry trade with Britain, and by the early 19th century more than 500 wineries were exporting sherry. Sherry has always been a favorite drink of Anglo Saxons, and so it is not surprising that the Canadian wine industry, like those of South Africa, Australia and the United States, should have been quick to concentrate on the making of sherry.

Jerez was a Phenician trading post 1,100 years before Christ, when its name seems to have been Shera. The Moors when they invaded Spain changed the name to Scheris but it was the English who gave the first name to the wine of the district — Sherris. This Sherris when first pressed from the local grapes in southern Spain was regularly treated with gypsum in a process known as "plastering." Legend has it that this stemmed from earlier fermentation of these grape juices in alabaster jars, which were supposed to provide a superior taste. The reason is that the grapes around Jerez have a very low degree of acidity, and this has to be increased. Niagara grapes, on the other hand, are especially high in acidity.

This "king of wines" is so old and so revered that it is cloaked with an entire mythology. For example, true sherry tasters, it is said, do not need to roll the wine round in their mouth – they can judge its quality by using their nose only. How they can do this when the contents of two butts of sherry from the same harvest and taken from the same vineyard and kept in the same bodega in Jerez for the same period of time will produce two completely different brands of sherry, such as a fino and an amontillado, has yet to be explained.

Fino and amontillado are two of the seven principal types of sherry. They are fino, manzanilla, vino de pasto, which are all dry sherries; amontillado which is medium dry; and amoroso, oloroso and "brown," which are all rich and sweet. Of course, none of these terms apply to Canadian sherries, which generally break down into three categories, dry, medium-dry, and sweet. No Canadian sherry is nearly as dry as a Spanish dry sherry. If it was, it wouldn't sell. The Canadian generally prefers sweet wines, including sweet sherries.

Sherry is oxidised wine, which means air is allowed to come in contact with it. This could not be done over a long period without the addition of spirits to the wine, for otherwise the wine would quickly deteriorate and turn to vinegar. Sherry, it should also be pointed out, is a blended wine, whether made in the cradle of sherries in Spain or in Canada. There is no vintage sherry with labels showing the year that it was made. This is because sherry making depends on adding wines of different years and because the longer this mixture of wines is aged, the better the sherry will be.

There are three methods now used for making sherry: the solera method, which is the basis of all Spanish sherry; the baking method; and the natural fermentation method. All three systems are used in Canadian wineries, and sometimes there is a combination of the first two.

Under the baking system, the wine is kept at 140 degrees Fahrenheit for two to four months to produce a base wine for sherry. This is often done by passing steam coils through the vats to keep the temperature high and even. In some instances, this baking can go on for as long as a year. The baking method, called the Tressler method for Niagara winemaking, combines the caramelization of the sugar in the wine with the release of oxygen to it. These effects, plus the addition of alcohol, produce a distinctive sherry taste to the wine and give it a high alcoholic content. The colour also increases during baking. During the baking process, taste samples are taken almost daily, and it is these which decide when the baking shall end. The wine is then cooled, racked, and then may be aged.

One of the principal advantages, however, of the baking process is in aging sherry quickly, so the general rule in Canadian wineries is not to age it for long periods in bulk or bottles after baking. But blending of different baked wines does take place because, though the baking process is used to produce the cheaper priced sherries, there is no wine where uniformity of taste is so consistently sought by the buyer. It should be added that not all baked sherry falls into the lower priced category. Some of the best sherries sold in Canada have gone through a baking process, but the addition of first-class spirits to grapes of distinctive quality, plus some aging, are other factors in their making.

Still, time is usually essential in obtaining the very best sherries. This is best done by the introduction of the flor yeast during fermentation and utilizing the age-old solera system of Spain. Brights, for example, let the flor yeast work on the sherry for three years, and Parkdale's top sherries are aged in barrels for a minimum of four years, and usually five. Parkdale puts all its sherry down in barrels, whether the final product sells at $1.05 a bottle or $2.35.

Under the solera system, the fermentation proceeds with the flor yeast. When it is completed, alcohol in the form of wine spirit is introduced. This does not retard the growth of the flor, which forms as a film on the wine. The sherry matures in casks with loose-fitting bungs, which allow the air to enter and develop the flor. For this reason, sherry casks have to be laid out in airy positions, and in many Canadian instances they are actually placed outside in the open. As the flor develops, it imparts certain substances to the wine, which give it the distinctive sherry taste and bouquet. Finally, after the yeast has fulfilled its function, it turns brown and forms a sediment, leaving a relatively clear wine.

Now, for really good Canadian sherry, the wine has to mature. This is done in the solera, which consists of tiers of casks with tight-fitting bungs, filled with sherry of different ages. When sherry is drawn off for bottling, it is taken from the bottom row of casks. These casks are replenished from the ones above, and those from the row above, and so on, until the top tier, which is replenished with wine that has just been through the flor process. However, not more than half of each row of casks should be taken so that, ideally, there is a maximum of mixing, or blending, of wines of different years.

In 1967, a British judge ruled that sherry produced outside of Spain can only be sold in Britain as sherry if this generic word is prefixed with the name of the country of origin. Thus, Chateau Gai, which exports to Britain, calls its sherry Solera.

The definition of port, universally the second most popular dessert wine, is even more restrictive. By an Anglo-Portuguese treaty, no wine is entitled to be sold in England as port unless it has been shipped through the bar at the mouth of the Douro River at Oporto in Portugal. Even in the U.S.A. a qualifying word has to be used on all labels to show the place of origin.

Oddly, though Portugal is the traditional home of port, the type of port sold there is much lighter than the heavy, sweet, and sometimes "crusted" port, which has become, as least in fiction, an amusing appendage of the 19th-century English clubman. The reason is that the heavy, sweet drink is good for cooler climates, but generally too heavy for those living in hotter climates. Port, therefore, should be acceptable in Canada. Perhaps because of a lack of men's clubs, the heavy, dark red drink has never been as sought after and only the lighter red port style wine is popular; particularly the light red port was popular before and during Prohibition days, possibly due to its sweetness and alcoholic content – but not in that order.

This sweetness results from the basic differences in port and sherry manufacture. Spirits are added to port wine before the end of fermentation when a high degree of sugar content from the grapes still remains in the liquid; with sherry the spirits are added only after fermentation is over – or, at least, near its end. One cannot be too dogmatic on this point because the times of adding spirits with both port and sherry depend on the degree of dryness or sweetness required in the final product. Again, port can be made by a baking method and can be improved by long storage.

The traditional types of port are tawny, which is slightly dry, has been fully aged in the cask, and does not improve in the bottle; ruby, a blend of tawny and a fresh, young wine with a fruitier flavor than tawny; white port, which is actually amber-colored and very sweet; vintage port, which will improve in the bottle up to 40 years; and crusted port, which is usually a blend of vintage ports. Canadian wineries do not list their ports in this way. All the ports they produce, with the exception of one or two, are very sweet, and this means that there is not the necessity to put as many brands on the market as is necessary for sherry.

There is even less need for variety with vermouths. To date, the world has been content with sweet and dry vermouth, a word derived from wormwood, the shrub whose flower was used for centuries to flavor the wine to give it its distinctive taste. As wormwood is no longer used, Canadian winemakers make the wine aromatic by steeping it for about a month in large tanks containing various plants and herbs. This takes place before fortification by spirits. Again the timing of fortification depends on whether a sweet or dry vermouth is required.

With all of these fortified wines, indeed with all wines, the buyer can easily tell the sweetness of a wine. A few years ago all Ontario outlets for wine adopted a sugar content code. It is now being copied in many other Canadian provinces. The code numbers are always listed in these outlets, but because so many buyers seem to have missed them, they are worth repeating. If the code number given against the listing of the wine in government liquor stores is zero or one, it is very dry; if it is two to four, it is a dry wine; five to eight is a medium sweet wine, and nine and over is sweet. As Canadian-made sweet vermouths range from 13 to 15, they can be considered very sweet.

CHAPTER TEN

Whites And Reds

IN British Columbia there are Riesling grapes growing on imported European vines in soil and climatic conditions as near as possible to those of their native land, but when made into a Riesling white wine the taste is completely different. We can even trace the genealogy of what John Vielvoye, the grape specialist for the British Columbia Department of Agriculture, prefers to call the Okanagan Riesling because of the different wine it produces.

Dr. Eugene Rittich came to Canada from his native Hungary in the 1920's after studying viticulture and wine chemistry and after years of work in the wine industries of several European countries. About 1930, he set out at an altitude of 2,000 feet a trial planting of 40 varieties of European vines on Black Mountain, ten miles north of Kelowna, B.C. From these, he chose ten varieties which seemed best adapted to Canadian conditions for commercial plantings at Ellison, which is also near

Kelowna. Among them was a Riesling. Dr. Rittich had imported the variety from Alexander Teleki, a noted Hungarian vine breeder, whose rootstocks, like Teleki 5BB, are still used in Europe and North America today. In 1935, Rittich became the wine-maker for Growers Wine Company and the Riesling vines began to travel to different locations in British Columbia. Another fellow Hungarian, Mike Barzel, obtained Rieslings from the home of Joseph Renyi where Dr. Rittich had planted them. So the Rieslings were now growing at Ellison, Oliver and Osoyoos in central British Columbia, Barzel passed on some cuttings to Mike Kerri at Penticton, Kerri let John Detterbeck have enough cuttings for three acres. Thus, this one variety multiplied throughout the Okanagan. Today there are 163 acres in that province growing this one variety. It isn't a figure that will send Canada soaring from its position of twenty-fifth to first in the world's tally of wine production by countries, but it does indicate how in a relatively short time, a few vines can spread.

The spread would have never taken place if it hadn't been for the Canadian's growing desire for good table wine. In the late thirties, few wanted what the Riesling could produce in British Columbia. The popularity of table wines – that is, wines to drink with meals – has been essentially a post-war development in Canada. In the case of Ontario, at least, this can be statistically proven. In July 1946, L. K. Brown, chief winery inspector for the province's liquor board, had every sales slip involving the purchase of wine checked throughout Ontario. He found that less than half of 1% of the wines bought were table wines. Twenty-two years later in 1968, 32% of wine sold in the province, including imports, was table wine.

It didn't matter in the earlier years of the century than a small wine grower, Nick Pataracchia, of St. Catharines, went back to his native Italy and won gold medals at Bologna for two white wines he had produced in Niagara, or that another Ontario maker, F. W. Baylis, won medals for both sweet and dry wines at the Wembley Exhibition in Britain during the 1920's. The public didn't care; it wanted wines with the high alcoholic content of the fortified wine.

The change to table wines has been due to many causes and resulted from many promptings. One of the greatest causes has been travel. During World War II, a generation of young people who had been brought up through their childhoods without seeing a bottle of wine went to Europe, and for the first time saw people drinking wine naturally and regularly with their food. They came back, not only as veterans of the forces, but, to a limited extent, as veterans of another life-style. This did not mean there was an immediate demand for table wines, but at last, there was a goodly proportion of the population who knew something about table wines, and occasionally bought them.

The continued affluence of the fifties encouraged this climate. More people travelled, and they travelled to wine drinking nations. On vacations they found themselves drinking wine cheaply at almost every meal. They came back to Canada and were converts, perhaps not to daily drinking of table wines but certainly to the purchase of a bottle when they were entertaining friends. This trend was even greater in the sixties, the decade when the buying power of the young made its mark. The sellers realized that those in their early twenties, and even those in their late teens, were the group with enormous purchasing power. Easy travel by jet aircraft, longer holidays, the importance of tourism to many national economies all meant these younger people were being drawn to Europe and its wines. They, too, returned home with a taste for wine at meals.

At the same time the immigration pattern to Canada had changed. Previously the majority of immigrants had come from Britain and the northern schnapps and beer-drinking nations of Europe. In the fifties and sixties, tens of thousands arrived from Italy, Portugal, Greece and other "wine countries." They continued their life-long habit and began making their own wine in the basement; they wanted wine, not water, at the restaurant table; they bought table wines at the liquor store.

These immigrants changed the way of life of cities like Toronto, which, as an example, now has more Italians than Florence, Italy. Other Canadians, native-born and of other immigrant stocks, saw what these new Canadians had brought to their environment, liked it, and adapted it.

However, this change in the Canadian wine-drinking preferences could never have taken place without the preparatory work of some devoted pioneers during the thirties and forties. They were the men of the Vineland Horticultural Station, of such major wineries as Brights, and of the government agencies, who believed that there was a future for table wines in Canada. There is a street in the small Ontario community of Vineland named after

M. J. Rittenhouse, a native of the small town beside Lake Ontario. Rittenhouse left the town and became a millionaire. In the early part of the 20th Century he bequeathed a large tract of land to the Ontario government for agricultural research. For some years the government did nothing with it. Eventually, somewhat embarrassed, the government set up the agricultural research station.

At first, most of the research was on fruits, but the grape was largely ignored because it so happened that one of the early directors of the station would never allow wine to pass his lips. This situation couldn't go on forever. The Vineland station was the only one of its kind in Canada. Grape growing was not only on the doorstep in the Niagara peninsula; it was an important part of the agricultural economy of the province. And, after Prohibition, wine made from Ontario grapes was bringing taxes into the provincial treasury.

There were, however, others on the staff at Vineland who were ready to impartially but enthusiastically apply their considerable scientific knowledge to help Canada get better grapes for wine-making. These individuals – and at least four, Dr. Lloyd Truscott, Dr. Angus Adams, Ralph Crowther and Ollie Bradt deserve mention – helped create a vast experimental program involving plant breeding, microbiology and testing, which would be the envy of any country. Indeed, it is recognized as such. One-third of all Vineland's food scientists today have come from Europe, Africa and other parts of the world because of its renown, and regularly delegations of scientists from overseas visit Vineland to see their latest work – for there are no secrets, no Iron Curtains on the scientific side of winemaking.

When you, Mr. and Mrs. Canada, next sip a clear, golden table wine with your chicken on Sunday or choose a Canadian red to accompany a rare steak in downtown Calgary, Halifax, or Ottawa, spare a thought for Vineland with its 300 name strains of yeasts (one of the bigger collections of yeasts in North America), with its tests to find out how increased use of fungicides on grapes may be slowing down fermentation on the average of 100 grapevine varieties checked on its testplots yearly. All of this work, which is only the slightest inkling of the volume of experimentation proceeding daily in the fields and labs of Vineland may seem remote from the glass, but has a decided influence on what goes into it.

For instance, the juice of a grape developed at Vineland is increasingly used in the blending of good Canadian table wines. There may be Concord juice in the same blend, as well as the juice of two or three other grape varieties. But 20 years ago, the chances are the table wine would have been pure Concord. The addition of the Veeport, essentially a product of Vineland as a vine adaptable to Ontario growing conditions, has resulted in an entirely different table wine.

This doesn't mean that the experimenters, the growers, the winemakers are now sitting back on their heels. Already the Vincent grape is being grown and finding its juice in the wine vat. Increasingly, this variety may be used for blending of better class table wines. And after the Vincent, there will be others, because the search goes on daily for the truly great wines that Canadians are likely to be demanding in the future.

The same type of trial and error approach has been applied over the years by the larger wineries since that watershed in the industry of the early 1930's when it was realized that Canadians could only be interested in buying native wine consistently and increasingly if that wine were improved. Brights, with its own 1,000 acres for testing and development, is an example. When Harry Hatch bought the company from the Bright family in 1933, the winery was making half a dozen not very good brands from native grapes. Soil in the Niagara Peninsula for grape growing was better than areas producing much better wines, climate was no worse during the growing season than in Germany, Austria, and much of France.

The difference was in the grapes. So a program costing several hundred thousand dollars, was started to see which grapes could be introduced from Europe or the United States, or whether by hybridization vines giving high quality grapes with distinctive taste, could be developed satisfactorily for Canada. The original budget was too low as the undertaking became ever more ambitious. Eventually two million dollars was to be spent by Brights and it was to take a generation of experimentation before Brights could claim to be producing high quality wines, and especially table wines.

At the start, people like Adhemar de Chaunac, whom the reader has already encountered, searched Europe for vines which might adapt to the Niagara Peninsula. Hybrids were developed, some in co-operation with Vineland. Each young vine was at first grown under glass, tested, discarded, or held for further experiments. This first stage could take up to four years. When a few grapes were harvested from a vine, they were made into wine, aged, tasted. Again many were discarded at this point because the resultant wine had a lack of clarity, bouquet, taste – or for one of many other reasons.

Altogether, in the past 30 odd years, 200 imported grape varieties have been tested by Brights. From them there have been 30 successes, vines which today are producing grapes of distinctive taste in the blending of wines. These "new" grapes to the Canadian scene were first used for the making of sherry and port, but soon after were finding their way into totally different table wines, sauternes and clarets and burgandies.

There were never enough, for the company couldn't rely only on its own acreage for production of these hybrids. Once proven, the grape growers had to be convinced to either pull out and replace their old varieties, such as the ubiquitous Concord, or to develop new land for the new hybrids. This is difficult. The man of the land tends to be conservative. However, economics eventually won (or have partially won) the grape grower. Immediately after the war, a grape growers' board was formed in Ontario to protect their interests. One of its aims was to ensure a ready sale for grapes at a fair price. This is achieved yearly when representatives of the grape growers and wineries sit down to bargain over prices; and now as the grower is paid twice as much per ton for the higher quality hybrids than the common Concord he has an incentive to pull out his old vines and replace them with new. So, today, Canadian table wines of all the major companies now are produced of blends containing a higher proportion of high quality grapes, like the Seibels, President, Pinot Noir, than ever before.

The supply can hardly meet the demand, and in rare cases, can't. At least one top quality wine made from the excellent Pinot Chardonnay grape isn't available everywhere within 50 miles of where it is made. Such is the change in drinking habits that when late in the 1960's there was a "beer strike" some smaller wineries sold out their own stocks. If the strike had lasted a few more weeks the whole industry would have faced a crisis.

Especially the young drinker is attracted to these better quality wines with food. "Burn, baby, burn" may have been a cry of the sixties, but it can only be associated with a miniscule part of their generation. In fact, the majority of the under-30's seems more identifiable with its criticism of the "burn, baby, burn" type of heavy alcohol drinking of their elders. It sees drinking as a pleasure, not an escape or a punishment, and in consequence seeks out the lower alcoholic content wines of the table. Nor are these younger, more sensible people much influenced by the inhibitions that have cursed wine drinking in the past. They don't worry about the foolish etiquette which (usually in non-winemaking countries) has proscribed that white wine can't be drunk with red meat, or a red with fish. They drink what they like, or in the words of the age, "do their own thing," and the devil take those who would make a fetish out of wine drinking.

CHAPTER ELEVEN

The Sparklers

Q UIZ question for your next party: if you had a bottle of champagne, neck down, with several months deposit of a sediment on the stopper, how would you get the muck out?

Answer: quick-freeze the neck of the bottle so that a plug of frozen wine containing the sediment can be disgorged.

It is appropriate to use a "party" question to introduce champagne because, more than any other wine, champagne is a "party drink." It can be drunk at any time; some people have used it at breakfast to cure the hangover of the night before. Others swear it should only accompany ice cream, and still others find it essential to seduction. To many, particularly females, it is the prettiest wine. To many it is the most mysterious wine. To many it is the finest of wines. There are few who can't stand it.

Champagne as we know it today is, in the long, storied history of wine, a comparative youngster —

a mere 300 or so years old. It is true that before the 17th century there was a form of champagne – any wine with a secondary fermentation in the bottle under pressure will create bubbles and pop when it is opened. The trouble was that these wines were completely uncontrollable, and instead of popping gently, they crashed open with fury enough to smother brides or ship-launchers with a thousand splinters of bottle glass. That type of wine was dirty too, from the sediment which clouded it.

Then came along the good Dom Perignon, a priestly cellar master, to introduce the cork, blend the best of champagne wines, and stabilize their energy. He was followed by a woman, Madame Clicquot, whose name still adorns a famous brand of champagne and who invented the degorgement process whereby the sediment in the bottle could be ejected, thus assuring a brilliantly clear wine.

These advancements happened northeast of Paris in Champagne, an area bounded by the towns of Rheims, Chalons-sur-Marne and Epernay. It is an area traversed by vineyards from which the famous champagne producers get their grapes, and pocked with chalk caverns (originally dug by the Romans when they invaded Gaul) where many of the makers store their wines. It is an area which produces 75 million bottles of champagne a year.

All the world's champagne was once produced there. Now, however, similar white sparkling wines made in several countries have come to be known as champagne. The French champagne producers have repeatedly tried to prevent the use of the word champagne, and have brought litigation against one Canadian company which produces champagne. The case has been before the courts for some years, and while the French were granted an injunction to prevent the use of champagne as a name by the Canadian bottler, the decision is being appealed.

A sparkling wine such as champagne is basically a blend of thoroughly fermented still wines treated with sugar to produce a secondary fermentation in the bottle. At least five years should pass between the time the champagne grapes are picked and the occasion when the cork is drawn to release the gases which create the effervescent bubbles. In Canada, champagne is produced by this "natural" method, and by the Charmat method. There are also wines sold as sparkling wines by the winemakers of some provinces which are, in effect, carbonated wines. These wines are artifically injected with carbon dioxide.

While sparkling wines may differ in the degree of dissolved carbon dioxide or atmosphereic pressure they may contain, they must be made from the highest quality grapes. This particularly applies to champagne. Both black and white grapes are used and, as in Champagne itself, the peerless Pinot Noir and Pinot Chardonnay varieties, which have been brought to the Niagara district in the past 30 years, are a notable constituent in blending the better quality sparkling wines.

Because it is essential that no damaged fruit be allowed into the crusher, the check on the grapes used for champagne is more stringent than for other wines. The high acidity of grapes grown in southern Ontario is especially suited to sparkling wine manufacture because the wines have to be of good acidity and not too high in alcoholic content. Ideally, only "free run" juice is used in making the wines which are later blended for the making of champagne.

These basic wines are simply good white wines. After fermentation is complete, they are allowed to settle and then fined. The wines then rest, or age, for at least seven months.

Now comes the process of making the blend or cuvee, which marks the zenith of the vintner's craft. He may have been able to analyze the properties of each of the different batches of wine in the laboratory but essentially he still has to rely on taste, sight and smell at this critical stage if a fine champagne is to result. Having determined the right proportion of each of the still wines necessary to make the cuvee, he now adds cane sugar, and the blend is racked into a small vat and special champagne yeast added. The cuvee should have an alcoholic content of about 11%. In addition it must be able to produce a final wine of good acidity, clean flavour, delightfully attractive light golden colour, and pleasant aroma. It is a great balancing act which requires constant change in the mixing of the original wines to be blended and repeated sampling. Add the complications which can result from the later addition of yeast and sugar, and it can be assumed that this is no job for the amateur.

The cuvee is stabilized in the vat and then transferred to bottles, which are tightly corked to withstand the pressure that develops from the secondary fermentation. The bottles are then laid on their sides and stacked ceiling high in a champagne cellar under carefully controlled temperatures. As the months pass away the sugar in the cuvee is slowly fermented away and the still wines in the cuvee are turned into a sparkling wine.

The best Canadian champagnes may be in these bottles for a couple of years or more, while other sparkling wines such as sparkling burgundy are kept in bottles for at least a year. At one winery alone, there are always 86,000 bottles of champagne undergoing secondary fermentation. Nor is the long period required simply for this; it is also necessary to allow the various wines making up the cuvee to subtly "marry" and so make a pleasant taste.

Bottles for champagne have to submit to a pressure of five or six atmospheres at 50 degrees Fahrenheit, which is equivalent to about 80 pounds per square inch. They have to be, therefore, of special design and very thick glass. In Canada, for secondary fermentation, they are capped with crown caps, similar to pop bottles.

When tests have shown that the champagne is ready for sale, the bottles are vigorously shaken to break loose such sedimentary particles as dead yeast cells from the inside surfaces. They are then placed in other racks, cork down, at an angle of 45 degrees so that this disturbed sediment may settle in the neck of the bottle. Then, every day for a month, cellarmen give each bottle a sharp quarter-turn to shake any remaining, clinging sediment downwards in preparation for the disgorging process. Incidentally, a good "turner" — an occupation of the wine industry throughout the world — can turn 20,000 bottles a day.

Now comes our party problem: how to remove the sediment. The bottles are taken from their racks and carried, in the cork-down position, to a freezing tank in which the neck of each bottle is immersed in a special liquid kept at minus 18 degrees Centigrade. The bottles slowly revolve 360 degrees in this liquid for about 30 minutes, during which time the wine and sediment is frozen solid.

The bottles are then removed, the necks washed, and passed to a "disgorger." He slips off the crown cap and the pressure inside shoots out the pellet of ice containing all the sediment into a box. Instantly he swings the bottle upright so that the loss of wine is negligible, and places it into the "dosage" machine. This machine is a complicated affair with spring clamps which press the bottles tightly against rubber stoppers which fit into the necks as the bottles are being held at an angle. The sugar having been used up in the secondary fermentation, it is now necessary to add a sweetening agent to the champagne. This is also done by the "dosage" machine. It adds a small measured quantity of syrup made of brandy and wine and tops up the bottle with a champagne made of the same cuvee as a replacement for any wine lost when the sediment was removed.

The champagne is now corked for the last time. A special machine squeezes the stopper of cork or plastic to about half its normal size and rams it into the neck of the bottle. The bottle passes to another machine where the cork is wired, and to another for labelling. Then the bottles are stacked again to bring out the flavour of the wine. All of this complicated processing, plus the long periods for fermentations, explain why a bottle of champagne costs more than most other wines.

The other method of champagne making in Canada is the Charmat method where, rather than deal with individual bottles for secondary fermentation, "bottles" of 500 gallons are used. In 1907, a Frenchman, M. Eugene Charmat patented his "Veritable Procede Méthode Charmat" after years of experimentation. His theory was a simple one. If secondary fermentation could take place in a single bottle, it could take place equally well in a glass-lined tank filled with wine equivalent to several thousand bottles. His method of bottling was a still simpler concept. The champagne produced by the Charmat method was drawn from the top of the vat leaving the sediment undisturbed at the bottom. The process eliminated all the handling of individual bottles, the loss of wine through disgorging, and the cost of bottles broken by extraordinary pressures during fermentation.

In 1928, the Chateau Gai Wine Company bought the exclusive use of the "Méthode Charmat" for Canada, and has continued to use it ever since. The giant tanks, bottling, corking and wiring equipment were shipped from France at that time for the early production of champagne by this system in Canada. Since that time, because of increased demand new tanks, styled on those originally imported, have been added.

The actual making of champagne by this large-bottle concept is precisely the same as in other wineries where secondary fermentation takes place in individual bottles up until the time when a cuvee is chosen. That is, the grapes are gently pressed, the juice inoculated with yeast cultures, stored and racked several times, until there is a suitable base wine ready to be added to others as blend in the Charmat tanks. Then, after fermentation by this process, the sparkling wine is placed in individual bottles, carefully corked with hand-made Spanish corks, wired and is ready for shipment.

Which method produces the best wine? The arguments are endless. The Charmat method produces large batches of sparkling wine of uniform qualities. The bottle fermentation system is bound to result in variations because of the slight difference in dosage when spirits and syrup are added. But the Charmat route is undoubtedly more economic.

Either way, the beauty and the action are immediately evident once the bottle is open. For many people there is no more attractive sight in the whole range of wines than a sparkling wine, lively and colourful in a well-made glass. It doesn't matter to a woman that the crackling rosé she so admires only has 15 pounds pressure per square inch compared with champagne's 75 or 80 pounds. It is the gentle pink colour which has primary allure for her. It doesn't matter to the man that a sparkling burgundy may never have aged as long as champagne. His acquired taste – the deep ruby color, and again the bubbles, make him its booster. But for others there can only be one sparkling wine – the aristocrat – champagne.

CHAPTER TWELVE

Other Canadian Wines

" OH, to be one's own Minister of Internal Affairs" has been a heart cry of the Polish epigrammist Stanislaw Lec, but in fact, through the centuries, people have been striving – and succeeding in being so. Their stomachs have received every known animal and vegetable product in the search for sustenance and new taste sensations. Every conceivable flower and fruit, vegetable and bark has been tried as the basis of wine. Today, in the twentieth century, the search goes on, although in small measure.

Generally, the grape predominates. Certainly, in large-scale, commercial winemaking, it has no substitute. Only the grape has such good yield of juice combined with adequate sugar content and acidity to produce an astonishingly subtle gradation of tastes and colours. However, the grape is not cheap and abundant everywhere, so the cottage gardener and rural housewife still make home-made wine from other products – parsnips, rhubarb, potatoes and elderberries. And, around the world, there is a small commercial output of wine from pomegranates, oranges, dried fruits, grapefruit, pineapples, and a few nuts.

Canada is no exception in the non-grape wine field. There are New Brunswick blueberry wines, Ontario fermented cherry and honey wines and in British Columbia a choice of strawberry, raspberry, loganberry and apple wines. It's all a matter of public demand.

In 1929, two Chinese wines called Ngkapi and Muikwailu were available in Ontario liquor stores. They are long forgotten because their buyers died or switched to something else. In 1970, some of the maritime provinces have only a small offering of berry wines, but in Saskatchewan there is a big demand.

Of wines made today from products other than the grape, those created from honey would seem to be the most difficult to create because their base is so far removed from the juicy fleshiness from which we expect good wine. In fact, honey wine, or mead as it was then known, was the commonest alcoholic drink in England before the Norman invasion, and was still popular enough to be the miller's tipple in Chaucer's Canterbury Tales. Mead, indeed, was the usual drink in all the northern European countries where grapes could not be grown, and the special delight of the Celts. With the growth of transportation methods and the freer movement of people, mead was largely replaced in these countries by grape wine. Still, it has always had its disciples, and it is not too surprising to find that one Canadian winery, the London Winery of Ontario, has found a ready and growing market for its three varieties of honey wine in recent years – especially among women, who like its sweetness and colour.

The next time you see a bee sipping the nectar from a flower in your garden, you might remind yourself that it has 29,999 more flowers to go before it has collected sufficient nectar to make one bottle of honey wine. The bees, of course, that usually produce the raw material for this wine are in hives. London Winery contracts with many beekeepers for their product. Then, having received the honey, it has to induce many of the properties of the grape to make good wine. The sugar content is there in high degree, but yeast, acid, and a dash of sulphur dioxide all have to be added. With these additions, the making of honey wine is not unlike that of grape wine. It is allowed to settle for several weeks, is racked, filtered, aged for some months in sealed tanks, racked again, "polished," and bottled.

When Tommy Stokes first became a salesman for the Growers Wine Company in Victoria, he needed to cut a small pine and tie it behind his "tin Lizzy" to act as a brake on some of the hazardous interior roads of British Columbia. But it is because of men like Stokes in the late 1920's and 1930's that there are valley towns today where berry wines are the most popular drink. For Growers, and later Calona Wine Company in Kelowna, initially began their businesses with wines made from berries and apples. Today, berry wines are still a substantial part of their business, so much so that these companies can point to certain areas and peoples who are particularly heavy drinkers of these wines. Among them are the Doukhobor settlements around Nelson, the Ukrainians in the small northern Alberta towns, both men and women in the mining centre of Trail.

The fruitiness of these berries, and especially the loganberry, which is carried over into the wine seems to be the main reason for this popularity. Of the average British Columbia crop of 500 tons of loganberries, Growers Wine Company takes more than three-quarters yearly for its wines. A small amount has been exported to Britain, but unless the crop yield were greatly increased export business could not be developed far; domestic needs are too great.

This one company has not only produced sweet and dry loganberry wines and a brandy made from loganberries, but also finds lots of customers for its raspberry, strawberry and cherry wines. It also has developed a crackling rosé wine from raspberries, which, like all rosés, is a favorite with the female sex.

Not one of the Capozzi family, who own the thriving (and sometimes boisterous) Calona Wine Company, is named Jack, but it is a name looked on with affection by the company's principals – and, it appears, by the public. The company, when it was first trying to make an impression during the Depression, started by making ports and sherries with apples. The result was unpalatable wines with high tannin and low acidity. The public didn't buy them, and the company switched to grape wines. But the sixties have been a different story for the Capozzis. Their sales of grape wines bounded ahead, so they started to look around for new products.

One day a few years ago, a manufacturer of apple

juice and apple sauce, called Tom Capozzi, the son of the firm's founder, and told him some of his apple juice was fermenting. As Calona was in the wine business, could they use it? Tom agreed to make wine out of it. His father was disturbed. He remembered the disasters of the early years. Nevertheless, Tom went ahead, maintaining there was a market for apple wine provided it was promoted properly. He promptly named it Apple Jack – and ran afoul of the dictionary.

Webster's defines apple jack as distilled apple brandy. So, said Food and Drug Act inspectors, you can't put that name on a label for a product which is wine. The Capozzis bowed to lexicography, and changed the name to Double Jack, spelling out on the label below that it was an apple wine. It was either too late or the customers transposed the words; throughout British Columbia today it is still called Apple Jack – a wine with a distinctive apple taste with a distilled additive to bring it up to 20 per cent alcoholic content, which is the legal limit for wines. Forty thousand gallons were sold in the first year it was produced, 100,000 gallons in the second.

The Capozzis decided to hold four jacks. They added Grape Jack, Cherry Jack, and Berry Jack, which is made of loganberries, and these three are now accounting for sales of more than a quarter million gallons yearly.

There are three other classes of wine, apart from mead and the fortified berry wines of British Columbia, made and sold for Canadians. They are flavored wines, kosher wines, and sacramental and mass wines.

The flavored wines were first introduced in 1964

and immediately developed into a craze. First one, and then another winery produced flavored wines. They had names like Zing, Riki and Tini, and their reputation spread like wildfire. Usually juniper-flavored, their soaring sales for one or two summers cut into gin sales in Canada. Yet there were some wineries, like Barnes, Brights and Chateau-Gai, which refused to jump on the bandwagon, just as there were some provincial liquor boards who refused – and have always refused – to list them. These wines sold at prices comparable with minimum-priced ports and sherries, however, the Nova Scotia Liquor Control Commission eventually decided to double the prices of the flavored wines it was selling. This acted as a deathknell and as quickly as the craze had developed so it subsided. The public simply returned to their regular white and red wines – or back to gin. Today, there are still limited sales of these flavored wines, but it is unlikely that the bonanza days of 1964 and 1965 will ever return.

The kosher wines are prepared for the nation's orthodox Jewry by two of Ontario's biggest wineries. The process is similar for other wines in nearly all respects, but it has to be supervised by a rabbi, who receives $50 a day to ensure that the product is not touched by human hand or in any other way processed contrary to the tenets of the Hebrew faith.

A similar supervision is applied to mass and sacramental wines. Indeed, the stringencies are greater. Three pages of the Collectio Rerum Liturgioarum describe precisely how an altar wine for Roman Catholics shall be prepared and a further five pages outline the method in which it shall be

offered. It covers all exigencies, including what to do should an insect get into the chalice.

There are other bases for the making of these wines. The Practical Church Dictionary defines altar wine as wine with an alcoholic content of between five and eighteen per cent – a very wide range, covering everything from the lightest of table wines to the fairly well fortified dessert wines. And an official church decree is even concerned about the morals of the winemakers: "Let them see to it that in all dioceses . . . there be some fit persons who are above all suspicion, especially religious, of either sex, from whom the rectors of the churches may secure . . . matter for the sacrifice and sacrament of the Eucharist, such as can be used with a safe conscience."

Such are the proscriptions for wines sold in Canada in gallon jars to church supply houses and, in smaller quantities, through liquor and wine stores under such labels as T'agaste, St. Augustine and St. Austin. T'agaste was the birthplace in North Africa of St. Augustine, the author of the famous Confessions. It bears on its label an official approval, thus: "The wine in this container has the ecclesiastical approbation of the Bishop of the Diocese of St. Catharines, Ontario." – the diocese where the grapes are grown, the wine is made, and the product bottled.

One Ontario winery which has been making mass wine for 30 years is now annually visited by an Augustinian monk. He blesses the fruit as it passes into the winery, carefully inspects the preparation of yeast cultures, and regularly takes readings of sugar and acidity levels. He reports directly to the

St. Catharines Roman Catholic bishop on the suitability of the wine for mass, but as unerringly as the tide waits for no man so man must wait for suitable wine. While T'agaste, a light wine requires only a year for aging, St. Austin, a higher alcohol mass wine made from sun-dried grapes, is in wooden casks for three to four years before bottling. The monk must make many visits to the winecellars, a temptation for man, a temptation that must be spurned by a man of God.

CHAPTER THIRTEEN

Out
In The Vineyards

ALL Canadian wine, white or red, sparkling or still, grape or berry, depends on the winemaker's experience and the scientist's acumen, but without the grower's devotion for at least part of every day there could be no wine.

There are nearly 1,500 grape growers in Ontario, another couple of hundred in British Columbia. Some farm a few acres beside their peach orchards or chicken ranches, others have hundreds of acres bearing nothing but grapes. Some are third and fourth generation grape growers; others have arrived from Italy in the past ten years, worked a few years in home construction or the nickel mines of Sudbury before obtaining sufficient capital to buy a small vineyard.

In Ontario, the grape has been estimated to be responsible for industries with a value of $600 million of which $50 million is the actual value of Ontario-made wine which is consumed each year. Altogether, Ontario vineyards cover 22,000 acres and produce an average of 60,000 tons annually. These grapes are of 40 different varieties and have resulted in a swing in drinking habits so that of all the wine now consumed in Canada, 65% is now made in wineries situated between Truro, Nova Scotia, and Victoria, British Columbia.

Canadian grape growing, in its tiny 19th century beginnings, was little more than the hobby of small farmers scattered through southern Ontario. By the beginning of the 20th century it had become concentrated on larger acreages below the escarpment and bordering Lake Ontario in the Niagara Peninsula until, by the half-way mark of the century, virtually all of the province's grapes came from this one – by Canadian dimensions – small area. This trend has now been reversed in ten years. Nearly 40% of the grape acreage is outside the sheltering barrier of hills, which is such a marked physical feature of the Niagara Peninsula. Where air drainage is good the risk of frost damage in these "new" areas hasn't been as great as feared. Even in California, it should be pointed out, there is a risk of frost, although it usually comes earlier than in Ontario.

The grape grower is being forced out of the Niagara Peninsula to some degree by the acquisition of the land for roads, homes and industry so that Keith Matthie, secretary-treasurer of the Ontario Grape Growers' Marketing Board, believes that the last fruit grower in the area is likely to be a grape grower because of the already proven success of grapes on the escarpment.

But that day is far away. Long before, new grape varieties will have been developed for growth in other parts of the province on a large scale. Probably this will mean a return to Pelee Island and other sections of Essex county near the city of Windsor, along the shores of Lake Huron, and possibly even as far north as the Ottawa Valley. But with the labrusca vines given a good yield for 22 years and some return for much longer, the farmer who has planted these in one area of the province is not about to suddenly literally pull up his vine stakes, buy land in an untried area, and attempt to prosper with as yet unknown varieties.

The transformation will be a relatively slow one unless the demand for Canadian wine multiplies many times in the next few years. This eventuality, bearing in mind the rapid growth in consumption during the past decade, cannot be discounted.

In any case, the scientists have their eyes carefully cocked to the future. New methods of air circulation and warming other than the costly smudge pots and beating of the air by helicopter blades, are under study. Experimentation in growing practices are part of the daily work of the Vineland station. Mechanical means are now available to meet the labor shortage.

For instance, one current experiment at Vineland deals with the spacing of vines six, eight and ten feet apart in rows which themselves are six, eight and ten feet apart. The object is to find out whether an increased yield per acre can be expected with these high densities of plantings, whether the soil can support this intensity of growth, whether the vines will get sufficient sunshine, and whether they will serve to protect each other. If greater crops are proven by these tests, it is but the first stage. Grape growing machinery would then have to be redesigned to operate within rows only six feet apart. It really means a balance of the advances of agricultural science against economics. The grape grower has to weigh whether the returns from increased crop yields would be sufficient to outweigh the heavy capital costs of replanting vines and buying new machines. His costs are great enough already. An Oakville grower, in the latter part of the 19th century, gave the costs of planting his vineyard as $148.50. Manure accounted for $45 of this, 300 posts for his trellises at 10 cents each meant another $30 bill, while 300 Concord vines cost him $24. Even in the 1930's, good land in the Niagara Peninsula could be bought for two hundred dollars an acre.

Today's costs are very different. Apart from the capital cost of the land, the Ontario farmer spends $500 an acre setting out his vineyard with roots, posts and wiring. He cannot expect a good yield until the fourth or fifth year. In British Columbia, irrigation is an added burden, apart from the initial expense for pumps, sprays, and water lines, it costs a further $300 an acre to water the vines each year. In fact, these high basic costs have, and will continue to benefit, the wine drinker. The cost of planting hybrid or vinifera vines, with their better quality grapes for winemaking, is only slightly higher than more common vines. But the price paid by the winery is as much as double for the better quality grapes than for the basic Concords. Indeed, it has been argued that these grapes could become a marginal crop. Surveys have shown that it now costs the Ontario grape grower $300 to $400 to produce an acre of grapes each year. He can expect an average of four tons to the acre. And, in 1969, the price paid for Concords was $120 a ton.

The minimum prices for grapes are set by negotiation. The negotiating committee is comprised of three representatives of the Ontario Grape Growers' Marketing Board and three representatives of the processors, of whom two are appointed by the Canadian Wine Institute and one by the Ontario Food Processors' Association.

The grape growers board was formed in 1947 after two groups representing the eastern and western divisions of the Niagara Peninsula had failed to work together for the benefit of all. The new board was none too soon in being formed. Even in the 19th century there was evidence that the grape grower wasn't happy. Two Canadians, George and Ben Chaffey, left their country, worked on irrigation developments in California, and then, in 1887, moved to Australia. There, they were so able to interest the state governments of Victoria and South Australia in their schemes that they received aid in developing two large tracts by irrigation so that, in time, they became two of the major wine growing areas of that country.

In the Prohibition period, of course, the grape grower was making vast profits. In the Depression, the "boom-and-bust" pendulum had swung the other way; he was getting $12 to $15 a ton for his grapes. Nor were the wineries always friendly. White grapes, in the 1930's, carried a $10 premium for each ton supplied by the grower. So the wineries introduced a cold press method whereby they could make white wines from red grapes.

Despite these sometimes difficult times, many of Ontario's grape growers have been there a long time. Bill Vaughan is an example. He has been on the same farm beside No. 8 Highway (which a future romantic government might some day rename Grape Highway) in Louth Township since 1919. He started in grapes in a small way — six acres of Concords. It wasn't until 1931 that he converted more of his farmland to vines, selling at first to one winery, then a group of them, and for the past 25 years to Brights. His first Concords were attacked by mildew, and the Forestry Worm went after his Dutchess crop. Other varieties have suffered from "wet feet" and have had to be pulled out. But, looking back, he says he has never had a bad crop failure.

Bill Vaughan is a man who lives close to the soil. From the windows of his farm house he can look out on his now large acreage of vines, made up of ten varieties. In 1931 he would pay 10 cents a box for vine cuttings. Today, some individual cuttings cost 45 cents. Then he took his grapes to the winery in a wagon drawn by a team of horses, and received $25 a ton if he was lucky and $15 if he wasn't.

Those were the days when winters were too cold to contemplate growing grapes anywhere above the Niagara escarpment, when it was common to cut ice 18 inches thick from the old Welland Canal, when days of ten below zero were not uncommon. They were also days when post holes for the vines were gouged out at the going rate of a nickel a hole, and a good man could do 12 in an hour to make himself 60 cents, and when women pickers used to be paid by the hour. Now, all the pickers including some women who have stripped Mr. Vaughan's vines each September for the past 25 years, are paid piece-work. This can bring some tidy "pin money," especially for good pickers able to garner a ton of grapes a day.

But some things don't change on the Vaughan

farm. While fertilizers have replaced manure in most vineyards, Bill Vaughan swears by a mixture of potash and barnyard manure to provide the best crops – and maintains he can tell by looking at the vines of Niagara which have received the traditional fertilizer from the barnyard. Pruning is another unchangeable necessity of the Vaughan vineyard. It starts around December 1 each winter and proceeds through to March, with farmhands and the occasional "welfare" case wielding the secaturs, under the direction of Mr. Vaughan's son.

Perhaps those who decry the flight from the land should take a look at Niagara, where there are a large proportion of father-son operations of vineyards. Another son who works with his father is Paddy Davis. His father came from Ireland around the turn of the century, obtained land, felled trees, built a home, and married. The son is in close contact with the Vineland experimental station, works cooperatively with Chateau-Gai and grows the varieties that winery suggests (just as the Vaughans grow varieties suggested by Brights), is president of the Ontario Flying Farmers Club, and has an alarm by his bedside that rings if the temperature in springtime gets too low.

The Davis vineyards cover 50 acres, and grow 200 tons of seven varieties of grapes for the winery. It is a modern vineyard with, among other things, towers for circulating warm air should the temperature drop near freezing point during the vital blossoming and budding weeks.

Labor, and particularly the seasonal labor, which is often transient labor, required at grape picking time, is becoming more difficult to obtain in Canada. Brights on more than one occasion have interviewed 600 men to find 75 suitable as grape harvesters. Other wineries and vineyard owners have had no choice; they haven't had enough applicants for the jobs of autumn.

Mechanical harvesting may end this concern.

Already one vineyard near St. Catharines under the management of Ken Stewart has used a mechanized harvester to bring in the grapes. Instead of the 80 pickers employed previously, two men, two tractors and the harvester were used. The harvester, which straddled the grape vines, shook the grapes into a catcher, from which a conveyor transported them into bins and was able to harvest one and-a-half acres of vineyard an hour and thus "pick" 100 tons of grapes a day. This development may mean that soon the West Indians who are now flown to Canada to pick grapes and other fruits may no longer be one of the "sights" of Ontario in the fall.

There are now eight million vines to be picked by hand in the Niagara area, and the nurseries were selling between two hundred thousand and four hundred thousand new vines a year in the latter half of the sixties. Already, at the beginning of a new decade, there are indications that at least a half million new vines will be added yearly to help quench the growing Canadian thirst for the wines of the country. Machines must soon replace men, as in so many other industries if consumer demands are to be met.

CHAPTER FOURTEEN

Down
In The Market-place

THE newly arrived visitor to Canada tends to
deplore our drinking regulations. He should have
been here twenty years ago, or ten, or five, for we are
changing for the better. The rule of course doesn't
apply to all our visitors. Even some from Britain,
justly extolling the virtues of their pubs, have to
admit they close at 10:30 p.m. while in most of
Canada one can drink to midnight or 1 a.m. now
without seeking out a bootlegger or private "club."
And those from Germany, rightly praising their
beer gardens, have to agree that you can't sit in
them in winter. If the visitor should come from
quite a surprising number of the American States,
some of which have no drinking on Sundays and
many of which have other even more absurd stric-
tures on drinking, there is likely to be a different
kind of astonishment: They are surprised at how
"open" our regulations are, and how agreeably
civilized it can be to sit over a glass of wine, with
or without food.

This doesn't yet mean we live in the best of all possible worlds, but the inhibiting shadow of the past is receding; a long shadow because until fairly modern times, drink – whether a light wine or 70% proof spirits – has been evil.

The few who believed that the country was hell-bent because of the amount of wine, beer or liquor consumed have been powerful. It could be argued they have consistently mounted the most effective lobby this country has seen. Politicians of all stripes, editors of all beliefs, churchmen of all faiths, distillers, brewers, winemakers, saloonkeepers, advertisers, radio commentators, television station operators, to say nothing of the average populace, have gone in deadly fear of them.

Don't blame the 19th-century Victorians. This is largely a 20th-century phenomenon. In the last century there was a generally healthy atmosphere to drinking, interrupted of course by the occasional lengthy blast from the pulpit.

The young nation's first prime minister, Sir John A. Macdonald, was a reflection of his times. He drank openly. He was even known not to split hairs; to have been drunk. And he was reelected.

The new city of Winnipeg as much as the old one of Montreal had its long bars. Erindale, a tiny Ontario community, now practically a suburb of Toronto, but as late as the 1950's little more than a village street, once had its selection of taverns to serve the stagecoach passengers on the Dundas Highway. Only the province of Quebec had, for generations, something approaching sane laws. This used to mean that members of parliament and members of the press gallery nipped across the river to Hull when they wanted a drink. But this didn't help, because drinking of alcohol is controlled by the provinces, not by the federal government.

Throughout the land women were forbidden to drink in public through the thirties, the forties, and even into the fifties, or they were confined to a special bar – with escorts. (It is my belief that Banff owes its growth as a tourist resort to the fact that it had the one bar of this kind in Alberta, for years, and Calgary women, with their husbands or boy friends, were the main customers.)

During World War II, women on the prairies had their fur coats designed with an inside pocket large enough to take a bottle. Checkrooms at dance halls did poor business because the women had their coats draped over their chairs so the bottle could come out for themselves and their escorts, and go back again in case there was a police "raid." Or they could always drink in a hotel bedroom. Or, a decade later, in a motel. But not legally at home unless they had bought the wine or other beverage themselves. Unbelievable as it sounds, the only person allowed to drink from a bottle bought in a liquor store of many provinces was the purchaser. Legally, there could be no offering a guest (or even a wife) a drink in the neighborly wine-tasting fashion of the rural Canada of the late 1800's. The introduction of cocktail bars into Ontario changed all this, but very slowly.

Through the 1950's, in most parts of English Canada, it was still necessary to buy an annual permit for the right to buy alcoholic drinks. Even into the 1960's, a medical prescription was needed before a person could buy wine or anything stronger throughout the province of Prince Edward Island: It was illegal to drink in a tent in Ontario: and the police could arrest you for drinking a beer on your own lawn in many other parts of Canada.

In such a lunatic society, I doubt whether the following story is apocryphal: In the 1950's, a government-appointed commission started investigating the "liquor situation" in Manitoba. It held public hearings, and at one of these the Women's Christian Temperance Union presented a brief. Having done so, a member of the commission asked how many members the organization had. The reply was 28. "No," he said, "I asked how many members, not how many branches."

"That is right," he was told. "There are 28 members."

Even if it were 280, those 280 women had literally controlled the drinking habits of a million Manitobans for decades.

Now, of course, nearly everything has changed. There are still "dry" areas throughout the nation — there is even one in the western end of the city of Toronto — where voters repeatedly refuse to allow any form of outlets for liquor or restaurants to serve wine or taverns to be established to sell beer. But no longer do government liquor stores have to have their windows painted so nobody can look inside (the precise height of the opaque barrier was laid down in Ontario's liquor laws), nobody has to sign his name and address to make a purchase, and women can not only drink but in most parts of the country are no longer segregated from men.

The nation didn't embark on any orgies to mark these successive changes. In retrospect, it seems that only first fear, and then inertia, prevented the changes from coming quicker. But they have come, and each has helped to introduce Canadians in greater measure to their own wines.

As long ago as 1934, a government appointed committee was recommending in Ontario that wineries be permitted to advertise the qualities of their wines, and especially new products, to develop "the light wine trade" in the province. But little heed was taken – and, it might be noted, there has been a notable lack of success in some instances; for instance, in Prince Edward Island, 90% of all wine sales today are of the heavy alcohol, dessert wine variety.

Most provincial governments took a hypocritical view of all alcoholic drinks during the 30 years succeeding Prohibition. They wanted the increased government revenues from taxes on wines while doing little to help promote a civilized environment for their use. They deplored alcoholism, officially, but took few steps to prevent it. Now, Canadians live in happier times. Some of them would say miraculous times, bearing in mind the stringencies of the past.

Today, to take one province, there are 430 government liquor stores in Ontario alone; a far cry from those of the past. Then, they not only hid their interiors from the gaze of passers-by, but with guilt hid their wares inside. Not that there was much being offered in wines, just a few varieties on a central list in the store identified by code number, name and price.

The experience of a new English immigrant typifies those times. He arrived in Canada during December, found work, and went, a few days before Christmas, for the first time into a Canadian liquor store to buy some wine to accompany Christmas dinner. Shocked by the barrenness of the store, the lack of colour, the non-existence of bottles, he went to the clerk, and asked where he could select wines. The clerk curtly directed him to the liquor list. He went and finally found the usual paucity of information – number, name, price. As a former prisoner of war, he was reminded how he had been drilled in the services only to reveal to the enemy three facts, number, name and rank. He returned to the clerk to ask whether he had been directed to the right place; was that the "only information on wine?"

"Yes, sure," replied the clerk, still sourly.

"But I want to know which years they are," said the immigrant.

"Oh, just hold on a minute," said the clerk sarcastically, "I'll go off and phone France."

The average liquor store clerk perhaps today can't give precise information on vintages of imported wines, but he won't be brusque and he will have a lot more wine information than his predecessors of a decade or so ago. This is because education has become an important part of the new "climate": Liquor boards themselves, in some instances, have set up programs to acquaint their staffs with wine, and the Canadian Wine Institute organizes courses on wine for hotel and restaurant staffs. They are certainly needed. As recently as early 1970, the first Canadian Travel Congress was held in an attempt to bolster tourism to the country, and the main complaint of representatives of the travel industry were that current drinking regulations were unsatisfactory for the overseas visitor and that the

service supplied by too large a number of hotels and restaurants was poor.

They might have specified that, particularly outside two or three main Canadian cities, the attitude to wine with meals is abominable. This especially applies to Canadian wine. Many hotels and restaurants, although having the licences to serve wine with food, have a poor range of wines, inadequate storage facilities, and refuse to learn the qualities of the wines they do sell, while charging exorbitant "mark-ups." This particularly applies to Canadian wines when they are available. There is no uniformity. One outlet in Niagara Falls sells a wine which is made in Niagara Falls at 200% more than its price in the government liquor store just around the corner while the leading hotel in Ottawa, 400 miles away, sells the same wine at only 100% profit.

The 200% markup over the set liquor store price is not uncommon in Canada (there are instances where it is higher), and because a 200% profit on higher priced imported wines means more in the till than the same markup on a Canadian wine, many hotels and restaurants either don't stock the Canadian products or do so in very limited quantity and range. Waiters often reluctantly reveal that there are such native products on the premises.

There have been suggestions that "kickbacks" are made to hoteliers, maître d's and wine waiters to stock and generally promote certain wines. If this is happening it shows why many officials of the Canadian wineries are reluctant to see wine sold with less government control in such places as grocery stores. The late Gordon Gilbride, a president of Parkdale Wine Company, was one of those who believed that the sale of wine from grocery store shelves would not only be uneconomic but, like others, had evidence that where this practice had been introduced in some American states "payoffs" had been made to carry sub-standard wines, and a criminal influence was never very far away.

Fortunately, the Canadian wine industry is only dependent on sale of its products in hotels and restaurants for a very small proportion of its total bulk. Unfortunately, the hotel and restaurant are the places where the stranger to wine, and this includes the growing percentage of young Canadians, first meet it. If the wine is poorly treated and of high price, an immediate antipathy is created.

At official state dinners in Ottawa, there was for years a reluctance to serve Canadian wines. In the year of Canada's centenary celebrations, it was only after considerable lobbying by Canadian wineries that Canadian wines were made available in the restaurants attached to the Canadian pavilion at Expo. One official answer to the reluctance to serve this native product was that its price would be considerably less than imported wines, and so the wine would be considered no good.

If you travel within Canada, you are still not likely to find Canadian wines readily available. Not only do the hotels and restaurants ignore them or hide them, but the railways and airlines can hardly be accused of promoting them. On one trans-Canadian air route, the author was recently offered the choice of a French and Canadian wine with lunch in one direction, but only the French wine on the return. Although the basic cost of the French wine was double that of the Canadian, both sold for a dollar a "split" (a $6\frac{1}{2}$ ounce bottle) .

These circumstances affect the manufacturer. For instance, most of the wineries are not willing to bottle "splits," a situation that is likely to exist until particularly the transportation companies show a greater willingness to market them. In the same way, one of the major wineries withdrew the half-bottle size of one of its brands recently, although the half-bottle size is ideal for one or two people at dinner in hotel or restaurant, because by doing so it could get a "listing" for another of its products in the province's liquor stores.

At one time wineries used to sell wine by the cask so that it could be sold by the glass in hotels and restaurants. However, this practice, too, is decreasing, perhaps reasonably. Many outlets dislike this form of sale because without a heavy volume there is a risk of spoiling as the air gets to the wine, and consequent wastage. So, essentially, Canadian wine is aimed at the home. The wineries have been very conscious of their target: a middle-class Canadian who perhaps knows little about wine but is ready to be informed, who wants to drink enjoyably but moderately, and who wants a drink that is within his economic reach. Thus, the average Canadian wine is certainly of reasonable, rather than luxury price, and, it is an interesting corollary that this average price today, from $1.25 to $1.75, is about the minimum hourly working wage for Canada. In the thirties when wine was 30 cents a bottle, or in the immediate post-war years when it was 65 to 75 cents, the minimum hourly rates were also comparative to the price of wine.

What has changed remarkably in the intervening years has been the packaging of the wines. Even the miner's wife or the west coast fisherman now is likely to get his or her Canadian wine from British Columbia in a fancy decanter-shaped bottle, while in eastern Canada, one winery in particular, London Winery, sells some of its sherries in bottles moulded into the shape of wicker containers.

This is an extreme case of the influence of packaging, but it has paid off. This winery's prices are generally higher than the average because of the high costs of making its somewhat revolutionary containers (there are other fancy bottle designs, including one made of plastic), but the consumers — especially women — are quite willing to pay the extra money for an attractive container. Other wineries, although more modestly, have changed shapes, labels, even names, to lure design-conscious Canadians. "Eye-appeal" is now important because for the first time in a couple of generations, the buyer in many parts of Canada can now see a range of products in his liquor store, as well as in the wine stores of Ontario; he can pick and choose instead of blindly settling for a number and a name as in the past.

It all began at one downtown Toronto Liquor store where a display of wines was introduced. The liquor board officials were sure the bottles would be stolen within a week, but one senior employee, who was a proponent of the idea, was ready to meet any losses from his own pocket. The pilfering in the first year was negligible. The Liquor Control Board was convinced. Gradually it moved displays of wines into more stores and eventually 175 of its stores had displays.

Other provinces have followed suit. Saskatchewan stores now proudly point out the wines made in their own province at a small winery in

Moose Jaw. Vancouver and Victoria stores understandably give preference to British Columbia wines. Others almost equally share shelf space between Canadian and European wines. Now there has been a further development. First British Columbia and Saskatchewan, and now all provinces, have introduced some self-service liquor stores. Again theft has been minor. All the products in these stores, wines, liquors and imported beers are displayed. The customer helps himself, pays at a check-out counter. It's just like a supermarket, except there are no rebates on the bottles. (There used to be a 2-cent rebate on wine bottles up until after the second world war, but it was a cumbrous system and was discontinued.)

At least in the central provinces the bottles displayed in liquor and wine stores are generally of the 26-ounce regular size, although not in the western provinces where the gallon jug is still popular. It used to be common, too, in Ontario and Quebec, and was a better bargain than buying wine in regular-sized bottles, but the wine industry of Ontario, conscious of its often unwarranted association with get-drunk-cheap derelicts, no longer promotes wine in the larger containers within its own province. It is argued that the gallon jug of wine has only one stopping place – the bottom of the container. Six bottles present the same amount of wine but provide six stopping places.

In the same way, as a contribution to the efforts to eradicate what are euphemistically called in North America "social drinking problems," the same wineries are now attempting to have the alcoholic content of wines removed from labels and other literature so that the tiny segment of Canada's population which still buys wine for this property alone can at least be confused. At the same time, there are some individual grape growers and winemakers who would like to see wine below a certain alcoholic content – the very light wines – classified as food for a different reason – they want wine available in food stores.

The coming of more liberal laws governing drinking in Canada has brought with it a much more positive approach by the wineries themselves which not so long ago would only walk tenderly into new ventures for fear of repercussions. There are still restrictions on advertising, but at least there are now some ads on radio and in the press.

The 51 wine stores of Ontario, like the liquor stores, are brighter, sometimes glamorous, with displays of what looks like pink champagne (although it isn't) bubbling from the bottle or in the glass. One group offers a cellar kit – an attractive carton of the winery's leading brands of whites and reds and dessert wines so that Mr. Average Canadian can keep a small basic stock in his basement, just as the French Count de ---- does in his cellar or the Italian Barone - - - - at his hill farm. Another offers (it should sell well each Valentine's Day) the "Instant Romance" pack, consisting of a bottle of champagne, two glasses, candlesticks, a pair of candles and paper napkins. Everything, in fact, but the ring.

Grape growers, too, are now prepared to tell the story of grape growing and winemaking outside their stores. Displays have recently been mounted at such favorite annual exhibitions with the public as the Royal Winter Fair in Toronto and the Salon National de l'Agriculture in Montreal. Although films were shown at the French-Canadian exhibit, and booklets handed out on making wine at home, and although a display in Toronto depicted the fermentation and aging of wine, not one complaint was received in either province that the morals of old or young were being corrupted.

Indeed there are many who suspect that the wineries, and in greater degree the officials of various government liquor boards, have tended to follow, rather than lead, public demand. All hell would break loose, some averred, if wines were permitted with food in hotels on Sundays; with food in restaurants on the Sabbath; when drinking regulations were changed to allow drinking in bars until 1 a.m. on Sundays. In fact, as each of these changes was made there were few complaints; in some cases, none. Canada has grown up.

There are many who now argue that the country should go "all the way" and have "wide-open drinking." They aren't too specific so it is difficult to know precisely what they want. Certainly, Canada needs more outlets for wine, as well as other beverages, and this is especially true in rural and resort areas outside the big cities. Certainly, Canada needs better restaurants where wine is more readily available. It is true too that the Canadian's lot would be improved if, to quote one winery executive, "the greed of the politician and some hoteliers and restaurateurs could be diminished." But "wide-open drinking," if that means bars and restaurants open 24 hours a day, seven days a week, with an unlimited range of alcoholic drinks, including wines, is simply impractical and uneconomic.

What these advocates don't realize is that as far as wine is concerned, greater variety is available in Montreal, Toronto and Quebec City than in all but the larger capitals of Europe. Usually the comparison is made with the well-stocked liquor stores of New York, Chicago and Los Angeles. These, of course, are exceptions, as much as are the cities of the U.S. where there are no liquor stores.

In Canada today, about 900 imported wines and about 300 Canadian wines are available. Of course, that number of wines isn't available in any one province and there are still great discrepancies. In Ontario, for instance, there are more than 200 different Canadian wines for the buyer and more than 400 imported brands. On the prairies and in the maritimes there are far fewer, but it may be some compensation for those who live there that their provincial governments and liquor boards have always followed the lead of Ontario. This could mean that if they haven't got them already, the prairies and maritimes will soon have wine advisers in their principal liquor stores, and possibly may get a drive-in for boaters, where a bottle of reasonably priced Canadian wine can be bought to accompany their freshly caught Canadian lake trout. Ontario has one of these – at Port Carling in the Muskoka Lakes resort area.

There is a reason why there are nearly three times as many imported wines obtainable in Canada than there are native wines, although it probably has little to do with demand. In at least one province the average liquor board mark-up which means the provincial government, is 105% compared with only 64% on the Canadian wines it sells.

A breakdown of the price of lower-priced Canadian sherry, which in 1967 was selling for $1.05

a bottle, indicates how much of the wine drinker's spending goes to governments. The purchase price of the bottle of sherry from the winery, including freight and insurance and the bottler's profit, was 48 cents. A federal excise duty tacked on another 8 cents, and the 12% federal sales tax another 6 cents. This brought the total cost to the provincial liquor board to 62 cents. The basic selling price to the consumer was $1 so the liquor board's profit was 61.3%. But the government wasn't finished with the purchaser yet. There was also a sales tax of 5% in this province so he had to pay another 5 cents on the dollar and handed over $1.05.

Nevertheless, it cannot be argued that these taxes and high government mark-ups are a great deterrent to the wine drinker. In 1956, five million gallons of Canadian wines were sold; today, that figure has more than doubled. With such growth, the wineries can hardly begrudge some basic payments they, too, make to their provincial governments – $500 a year annual licence fee for operating a winery and $100 a year for every wine store they own.

Let us leave these statistics, which take the fun out of wine and to which, in all liklihood, the converted Canadian wine drinker never gives a thought, for we have slipped the bonds of the puritanical past. No longer can a wife have her husband put on a list kept by provincial liquor boards to which a man's name could be added without trial by jury and certainly without appeal, if his wife – or the liquor store clerk – maintained he was buying too much. In such a way he could be denied the legal purchase of wine, or any other alcoholic refreshment, which, of course, in the illogical way of the earlier part of the 20th century, sent him off to a bootlegger.

Gone, too, are the days when the *St. Catharines Standard*, a daily newspaper, in the heart of Canada's winemaking area, deliberately removed the word "wine" in all references to the Grape and Wine Festival, an annual celebration held in the Ontario city. As this festival has only been held since 1952, it is apparent how long the old thinking has prevailed. Now neither wine nor the festival can be ignored. The fact that there is such a festival similar to the great fiestas in the main winemaking countries of Europe, exemplifies the changes in attitude to wine in Canada. Wine has been brought out into the streets, at least symbolically, and is no longer a subject spoken of in whispers, or a clandestine drink behind opaque bar windows, or a package hidden behind a liquor store counter.

The ten-day Grape and Wine Festival held in St. Catharines each September, before grape harvesting and crushing and fermenting reaches its pitch, has managed to accent the happiness, colour, beauty and nobility of wine.

A Grape Queen is selected from beautiful girls of the small towns and villages in the vineyards of this region. A Grape King, is chosen from among the grape growers, as a tribute to the husbandry of these essential producers.

There are sports, wine-tasting parties, a ball, a dinner for growers and winemakers, bands (including a steel band from Port of Spain, Trinidad, a city with which St. Catharines has been "twinned" in 1969) and a parade. The parade does not accent so many cavorting Bacchuses or tipsily dandling half-clothed maidens on their knees, but instead brings out floats depicting various processes of grape culture and winemaking, as well as the other common denominators of any parade – drummers and marchers, music, laughter.

The festival now draws more than a quarter-million spectators, some of whom must go off to lunch and toast the fact that Canada has, at last, as far as wine is concerned, come to its senses.

CHAPTER FIFTEEN

We Even Sell Abroad

THAT thrifty lad, J. S. Hamilton, who, in the late 1800's, saved enough money to start his own Brantford store and then start marketing wine, was the first Canadian to export it in any quantity. In the early years of this century, his St. Augustine communion wine was sold throughout the West Indies.

Canada has only sent a small quantity of its wine overseas. Today its exports would hardly make a splash in the harbors of Bordeaux or Cadiz, through which the huge volume from France and Spain moves. This is not so much due to the quality of the wines but to two other factors: The native demand for wine in the past century has been big enough that the wine producer has had no driving economic need to seek out fresh markets. And the method of selling wines, especially in the logical market of Britain where individual wine merchants are wine specialists buying in bulk from the exporting countries and doing their own bottling, is strange to the Canadian producer – and a difficult system to "crack." All this has meant that Canadian wines have won recognition, even prizes, but rarely sales.

Both Paris and Philadelphia were bolstering the ego of Canada by lauding our grapes and wines in the 1860's and 1870's, and Toronto's John Hoskin, almost certainly the largest Canadian winemaker of the early 1880's, was able to report that "one gentleman of Birmingham" was prepared to take all of Hoskin's light port, and thought there were good prospects of selling it throughout England. However, the same middleman maintained it should be called Niagara, not port. Obviously, a born promoter. But there are no records of any further trans-Atlantic shipments. In any case, they could never have become large, for Hoskin, it is reported, used no press nor machinery of any kind, but had a man press the grapes with his hands "and rub them in the vat with a stick."

Another early optimist was Mr. Girardot of Essex County. He said, "I was born in France but I don't think there is any part of France where grapes bear so much or so well as in Essex County." In 1878, he took some of his wine to France to find that "French connoisseurs declared it superior to Bordeaux." Never at a loss for an unequivocal viewpoint, he put in an appendix, "I don't think that the wines imported from France to Canada are as a rule anything like as wholesome as ours because the foreign wine is doctored a great deal."

Medals in those days and even into the 20th century were the vogue at international food and beverage exhibitions. As late as the 1930's, a small Italian bottler in the Niagara was able to return to Bologna and nab one. Adhemar de

Chaunac produced a sauterne which won a "gold" in California, so to prevent any tarnishing of their own products by repetition, the Americans made him a judge for the following year. Vineland produced a yeast which enabled Canadian sherry, although only aged a year, to compete in Spain against that country's illustrious sherries, some 12 years old, and yet take second prize.

Canadian wines are still being "exposed" abroad through trade missions and food fairs; people overseas not only get a free taste but actually buy a bottle. Among the varied places where Canadian wines have been sampled recently have been food and drink exhibitions in Britain and Atlanta, Georgia, and trade exhibits in Seoul, Korea, and New Zealand.

There are still only two Canadian wineries which sell their wines outside Canada: Chateau-Gai, which was the first, and London Winery. Because Chateau-Gai puts considerable accent on its exports, the company has a distributor in Barbados where the wine is sold in a supermarket and in Great Britain where their distributor is romantically situated in a Sussex manor house.

A recent innovation has been a plan where Canadians can purchase the company's wines for delivery to friends or relatives in Britain. White and red and rosé wines, champagne and sherries are shipped in bulk to Britain and bottled and labelled there. Purchasers in Canada can order regular sized bottles or half gallon jars of most brands. In the first year of its introduction, more than 8,000 orders were taken in a few weeks for delivery of wines for Christmas. This type of sale, while not subject to the federal and provincial taxes and Canadian government markup, still has to be kept in proportion. Total exports of Canadian wine represent no more than a tiny fraction of 1% of the whole and are unlikely to increase greatly in the immediate future if home demands continue to rise. Without a vast increase in the grape acreage the wineries are going to be hard pressed to provide sufficient gallonage each year to satisfy the wine drinkers of the ten provinces.

However, there could be an exception to this prediction, as Canada already produces one great varietal wine in Brights Pinot Chardonnay; unfortunately, in very limited quantity. If the production of this wine could be increased it might catch the fancy of the overseas wine drinker. Alternatively, if Canada can produce, as the result of repeated testing by one of the wineries or the work of the Vineland experimental station, another great varietal wine in large quantities, it might become a great success in the export market. It might even be named "Niagara."

CHAPTER SIXTEEN

Making
Your Own Choice

PEOPLE drink different wines for different reasons. Jane Austen drank the South African Constantia because she considered it a cure for gout. The people of the Manitoba town of Beausejour, east of Winnipeg, drink the wines of the same brand name, made by Growers Wine Company in British Columbia, because they identify with it.

A very few drink a red Burgundy, Romanee Conti, bottled in 1929, because they consider it the best wine in the world. Even fewer drink a red Bordeaux, Chateau Lafite, laid down in 1864, if they can find it, because they consider it the greatest wine ever made.

Some Frenchmen like a wine of the Loire that has the aroma of violets. Greeks are happy with their native Retsina, to which pine cones are added so the resin will stop the wine from turning to vinegar, while some grannies in Eastern Canada still swear by homemade blackcurrant wine as a certain remedy for colds. A handful of topers in the metropolises of Canada have *mixed* port and brandy as an after-dinner drink.

A miniscule number are so possessive about wine they will let nothing contaminate it. I have sat during a luxurious dinner with a European who became one of Toronto's most notable restaurateurs; he literally only broke bread during the entire meal to accompany his wines. And there is the report of one mad connoisseur who carried four cardboard discs around with him which exactly fitted the tops of the four most common wine glasses. When he was out drinking, he would cover his wine glass with one of the discs to prevent the wine from being fouled by cigarette smoke between sips.

Some drink wine for its medicinal qualities. In fact, there seems to be a strong return to the belief in its curative values in North America. Several leading medical authorities in the U.S.A. have recently supported the value of wine because it is low in calories, acts as a tranquillizer, is good for digestion, and nutritional for diabetics.

A more surprising endorsement comes from a doctors' survey carried out on hospital patients, which was reported in the business publication, *Food in Canada*. This showed that 95% of patients who drank wine were satisfied with visiting hours and general hospital regulations while 57% of the non-wine drinkers were not; that all the wine drinkers thought their beds comfortable while only 50% of those who didn't take wine thought so; and that 85% of the wine drinkers liked hospital food while 43% who didn't drink wine thought the food was awful. One should not put too much credence in these figures; the wine drinkers may simply have been lazy, conservative, apathetic, or easily satisfied,

169

which are properties that could be applied to almost anybody, but they are at least as credible as the claims made for "eyebright wine" by a writer called Arnald of Villanove in 1310, "Wine from eyebright, euphrasia in Latin, is made by putting the herb into must, which then becomes eyebright wine. When such a wine is used, the eyes lose all uncleanliness and are rejuvenated. It also removes all impediments of the eyes and the defects of vision in all people, whatever their age and complexion is, whether they are by nature phlegmatic or fat. This has been testified by reliable people for while they were all unable to see without eyeglasses before, they were able to read small letters without glasses after its use."

Wine has always had an association with therapy; so much so that at one time in Hungary, municipal bars were restricted to selling wine "to those with fever, travellers and women in confinement." For years wine was listed in that "bible" of the American druggist, the *U.S. Pharmacopeia*. Of course, Prohibition put an end to that, and it has never since made a return performance.

Wine has been associated with medicine just as it has with religion because until very recent years it was such a mystery; nobody knew how it developed. Of all biological products, each of which has an astounding variety of tastes, wine had the greatest, so it was held in awe, like fire, by the pagans, because of its power. And the various religions, either by adopting it or rejecting it, have held it in awe ever since.

It is not inconsistent, then, that wine should have been featured in religious art through the centuries, nor that monks and priests should have been among the first and greatest winemakers, nor that since wine symbolizes the blood of Christ at the communion rail, the Last Supper should have been carved into the surface of one of the largest casks in the renowned Austrian wine cellar at Gumpold-skirchen.

There are others, for more secular reasons, who stand in awe of wine today. They are those who have been bludgeoned by "experts," snobs, and sharp salesmen into believing that the whole business of wine drinking must be accompanied by the right etiquette, the right protocol, and the right wines. These people are the worst enemies of all young wine countries, notably Canada. These know-it-alls are sometimes sophomores writing for university newspapers, whose great knowledge is based on 19 years of drinking "pop"; a few Canadians who after a couple of quick trips to Europe consider themselves to have been given a God-given authority on the grape; and some recent immigrants who still look down on "colonial" ways, particularly in regard to drinking. None of these could give the names of 12 brands of Canadian wines.

Grape growing and winemaking is an immensely complicated technological, scientific business that requires years of experience. There are only about a dozen people in the world who could rightly claim to be outstanding authorities on all facets of the two aspects so important to good wine. Additionally, when the yearly vintages of small individual areas of larger wine-growing regions are added to all the blended wines, there are tens of thousands of different wines. If half a dozen of these wines from all over the world and of different ages were poured, there are possibly only half a dozen wine authorities

171

who could tell precisely what the wines were and when they were bottled. And certainly the type of "experts" who proclaim so loudly in Canada, particularly when they have an audience in print, on radio or television, would have a hard time even naming the countries from which the wines came – and might even end up by praising one from Canada by mistake.

All of this is very bewildering to the Canadian who comes for the first time to wine. He should remember he is not alone. At three o'clock one morning in a hotel room in Tel Aviv, Robert Jay Misch, a secretary of the famed Wine and Food Society of Great Britain and a syndicated columnist on wine in North America, told me how he became a university lecturer on wine, too. Apparently his daughter brought home for dinner one night a young man from one of the 'ivy league'' universities in the U.S. During the course of the meal, Mr. Misch learned that not only did the young man know nothing about wine, but neither did any of his classmates, despite their superior economic and educational backgrounds. He asked the young man whether he thought his classmates would like to learn about wines. He thought they would. As a result, Mr. Misch approached Harvard and Yale and many other universities, and soon he was giving courses to the students throughout the U.S.

So the carpenter from Trois Rivieres, the bank clerk from Prince Albert, the nurse from Saint John is as likely to know as much about wine at the outset as the psychiatrist's son from Toronto or the university professor's daughter from Quebec City. This ignorance shouldn't lead to despair. Only a few guide rules are necessary to start enjoying wine. First, ignore all pseudo-experts and those with specious economic interests, like a few waiters who only "recommend' high-priced wines. Next, put the whole business of vintages on ice at least for some time. There are several reasons for this. Only two, at the most three, vintages of any wine are really great in a decade, so you run the danger of getting the right wine but the wrong year unless you become very knowledgeable. There are very few people with the knowledge and money to be able to regularly afford great first growth Bordeauxs, which even in Europe can cost $25 and more a bottle. In addition, you won't know which vintages will have travelled well – like temperamental children, some do it abominably. Dismiss from your thoughts all the paraphernalia of which wine with which wineglass or with which course, again for the time being.

Now, start buying and drinking different wines. At this stage, it is worth repeating that the Canadian industry only claims to make good wines and not yet to have produced great wines. The cheaper, non-vintage, imported wines in Canada are also good wines and, in my belief, better than the same wines under the same labels in their own countries in many cases. This would be logical. Most European countries are looking for export sales, especially in dollar countries, and are bound to ensure a good product.

For $10 you can easily get a bottle each of white and red wine, a dessert wine like sherry, and a sparkling wine. If you have never drunk any wine, this will be money well spent. It will give you an idea of four basic types of wine. You may prefer two of them. Don't be too adamant. If you don't like the sherry, for instance, it may be because it is too sweet. Try another which is dryer. You may find it more to your taste.

You still have a long way to go. There are more than 300 different Canadian labels alone to sample. That doesn't mean that you will; they aren't even all available in your particular province. But try a few more of each kind, and finally you will decide on the ones you really like. That is the most important thing in becoming a wine drinker. Why people who like steak aren't switched to lamb or why seafood fanciers refuse to become vegetarians while the same people can be so easily led from their preferences in wine by some single slighting remark is one of the conundrums of life.

So, in wine, as Shakespeare said it for all things "to thine own self be true," and to the wall with the snobs. This is not to say that you should disregard price entirely. Generally speaking, you pay for what you get with wine as for most things in life. If, at this stage, rather than keeping to one or two wines which you have found to your liking, you wish to be more adventurous and survey a lot of different wines, it may be as well to bear in mind a few rules of the professional wine taster.

Palates, it is generally agreed, although I don't think there has been any considerable medical research on the subject, differ greatly. Some people have very susceptible palates, others appear able to eat raw onion without hardly noticing it. We have already given one man's opinion that children should be the best wine tasters because of their active, unsullied, and untiring taste buds. There is a natural extension of this belief: tasters for European wine merchants usually do their work in the morning before their palates tire. This isn't always convenient for the average drinker. But it is possible that if you open a bottle for the first time late at night you won't appreciate it because you are tired. Moreover, by this time of the day, the taste buds are not only weary but the mouth is "unclean" – it is likely to have been subjected to a day's smoking as well as a variety of food tastes.

The cleanliness of the mouth is an important part of wine tasting. This means that if you are seriously trying to find out which wines you prefer, you should not try a new one immediately after tasting another, nor after certain kinds of food such as salads with a high vinegar content.

Another point to remember in this search for wines that you like is not to damn too highly a wine served in a restaurant or by a friend. It may have been stored near a hot water tank, which happened to a high-priced German Moselle wine served me in what is supposed to be one of Toronto's best restaurants. It may have been opened earlier and not properly recapped, so that it has deteriorated. Better give the wines in these circumstances the benefit of the doubt, and try them again some time.

If you are determined to know what you like (which is a far different thing from being either a pompous snob or a world authority), your main difficulty is that you are likely to buy and try individual bottles of wine over a long period. You will forget, no matter how good your memory, individual tastes. For this reason it might be worth taking a few notes on each wine. These need not be on colour, bouquet, body, and taste, which are the official wine-taster's basic criteria. You can work out your own rules as long as they are applied to all the wines.

Having now some knowledge of wines, having

made a miniscule selection from the vast array available, and having decided (at least within this selection) what you like, you may still be inhibited by all the marginal nonsense related to wine — when to cool, how to serve, how not to make an immense social gaffe, etcetera. Don't be.

The populations of the great wine-drinking countries of the world would never find the time to drink their 30 gallons a year per capita if they spent all the time on etiquette silly writers for the women's pages of North American newspapers maintain they should. These fatuous advisers obviously don't know that sangria, a national cooling drink in Spain, is a mixture of wine, ice and fruit. They have never seen the large number of French children and French adults who, not only in the privacy of their own homes, but at cafe tables, mix wine with water — despite the dictum. They don't realize that sherry on the rocks, while a nice drink, was deliberately encouraged to promote increased sherry sales.

This doesn't mean wine should be treated as cavalierly as the water every waitress in Canada brings to the table. At least give it as much respect as milk, which like wine has "body" while water has none. In fact, give it a lot of respect — but don't let it rule you.

You can, in the extreme, do what you like with wine, drink it from the bottle, leave it in the sun, have it for breakfast. I don't recommend this but, on the other hand, my own recommendations are very simply: Cool all wines except reds and dessert wines. Serve them in fairly large, clear glasses so the wine doesn't spill and the color can be appreciated.

This is a lot less than the basic one page of tips

given in the price lists of many Canadian provincial liquor boards which recommend that aperitifs, white and rosé table wines all be served cool at a temperature of 55 degrees, crackling and sparkling wines be served cold at 40 degrees, and red table wines and dessert wines such as port and sherry be served at room temperature. This doesn't mean that you walk around, worrying, with a thermometer, before the guests come for dinner. If you want a cool wine, put the bottle in the refrigerator for a half to one hour before serving; if you want a wine served at 40 degrees, put it in for two hours. As most homes are around 70 degrees, you won't have to worry about room temperature in Canada, and even if it is 73 degrees Mr. and Mrs. Brown aren't going to notice the difference in the wine, and neither are you.

The liquor board price lists, wine pamphlets, and other basic "guides" also present suggestions as to which wine should accompany which food. This originally had nothing to do with taste, but with geography. Germany, the home of the great white wines, has always had large supplies of fish, both salt and fresh water. Italy, most noted for its reds, has always had great supplies of grain from which the various pastas are made. The rich agricultural land of France has always had plenty of cattle and poultry for the meats, chickens and cheese which go with either red or white wines. (Perhaps some Canadian winery might like to extend and promote this natural relationship. I think there is no finer peach in the world than that grown in the Niagara Peninsula. On one occasion only I drank peach champagne, made by blending peaches and mixing with champagne. It was like nectar. A winery might consider investigating the possibility of blending both the grape and the peach of Canada into one bottled product.)

Necessity, and since, custom, has therefore decided which wines accompany which foods. Let us lay down the rules gently. First, champagne is allowed to go with anything, presumably because it costs more than other wines. It is generally considered a good accompaniment with ice cream and sweet desserts. All but the real nit-pickers will also allow that rosé wines can go with any kind of food.

Now we come to the parting of the ways. Sherries, particularly of the drier rather than the heavy, sweet "cream" variety, and vermouths are considered good appetizer or aperitif wines. A glass or two of these before a meal, rather than spirits or beer are supposed to whet the appetite, that is, reinvigorate the taste buds.

White wines are the usual accompaniment to fish and poultry; red wines are generally recommended to go with red meats, such as beef, and spaghetti and spiced dishes.

It is generally conceded that the crackling wines, as well as other sparkling wines than champagne, can be served with any foods, although sparkling burgundy, which is red, is often considered only "right" with beef, game or spaghetti.

Finally, the dessert wines like port and sherry are considered best at the end of the meal with cheese, nuts, fruit or cake.

The important thing about these recommendations is not to let them concern you. If beef is on the table and you only have a bottle of white wine, don't fret. The neighbors won't know. Your guests will prefer the "wrong" wine to no wine at all, and that only leaves yourself – and by now you are wise enough to know there really is no such thing as a "wrong" wine.

But there can be a wrong glass. It is usually green or royal blue or purple with a gold painted lip; diminutive so it can hardly hold more than a thimbleful of wine, with a knobbly stem so that it is difficult to hold. Wine glasses should be made for seeing the wine, smelling it, and drinking it, which means they should be clear so that the colour of the wine can be appreciated by the drinker and enhance the table; tulip-shaped so that the aroma of the wine is held in the glass at least to a certain extent, and large enough that a good serving can be put in them. It is not necessary to have a great range of different shapes and sizes.

Different glasses are available for table wines, crackling wines, champagne, and dessert wines, as well as the monstrosities. But in effect, one type of glass will do – it should be clear, tulip-shaped and hold six and not more than eight ounces. This type of glass should be only two-thirds filled at any one time. This is to not only prevent wine stains on the table cloth but to allow the bouquet of the wine room in the top of the glass.

Now you are ready. You have tasted a few wines, made a choice of those you like, obtained serviceable wine glasses, invited a few friends in, served the wine from the bottle. You sit down, the food is on the table, the wine shows off its beauty in the glasses, you take a first sip. This is one of the good moments in life.

CHAPTER SEVENTEEN

The End of the Bottle

In Canada an empty wine bottle is called a "dead 'un." The wine waiter in the restaurant is even more expressive; when the last drop has been poured he turns the bottle upside-down in the ice-bucket. It is a sad moment. A bottle of wine is a living thing. It is also a mark of man's genius.

As André Simon has pertinently noted, life on earth cannot exist without water; animals cannot live without water, man cannot live without water. But while all other animals have been content with water through the ages, one of man's earliest signs of his superiority to other beasts was when he made another more palatable drink, wine, which could also serve as a food.

That first wine was undoubtedly a very crude affair which we would not stomach today. But the son of the first winemaker tried harder, and may have soon been a better vintner than his father. So the progression has gone on as man has evolved.

The wine industry has wrongly been considered a

conservative one. It is true that where an outstanding wine has been discovered, there has been a reluctance to tamper with it so that, in the case of individual varieties, the only target is to produce a wine as good as the peer of years before, but these conditions only exist within a narrow frame of reference.

On a broader plane there have always been experimenters and these have given, over the centuries, new vines, the cork, the bottle, secondary fermentation for the making of sparkling wines, pasteurization, new methods of clarification, the modern scientific techniques applied to winemaking.

Starting in central Asia and northern Africa, these winemakers have spread out to the European continent and then, thousands of years later, to the ends of the earth – California and Chile, Australia and South Africa, Canada.

The grape farmer and winemaker of Niagara or Okanagan are the latest frontiersmen of this tradition. Sometimes in February, looking at these lands gripped by the dead hand of winter, it seems a miracle that they are there, but Canada is a land of great deceptions. Those feet of snow not only hide huge reservoirs of oil and stockpiles of minerals but rich soil for wheat or viticulture.

This country has been dismissed as nothing but several thousand square miles of frost and there are the uninformed today, easily deluded by a map, who consider it only a land of forest and lakes. They forget, or probably have never learned, of the stunning vastness, and the "pockets" of rich soil well suited to the growing of vines which are as large as several English counties or many departments of

France. It was to this land that the first Canadian growers came, and that was only a hundred years ago.

In that one hundred years, Canada has changed from one of the last of the great, old geological, uninhabited wastelands into a nation whose population seems set to double each half century. In that same one hundred years, Canada has become a "wine country," a term that requires elaboration, a title which deserves to be put into perspective.

In this year of 1970, at the great annual wine fiesta at Jerez de la Frontiera, Canada takes pride of place – for the first time recognized as a wine producing country. It is an indication that the global wine trade, as represented by the sherry makers of Spain, recognize that Canadian wine can no longer be ignored. But this doesn't mean there will be a great clamoring at the ports of Halifax and Montreal for Canadian shipments; there are many major wine-producing areas of the world whose produce is primarily for home consumption, nor can it mean that Canadian wines are rated with the grand crus of France or the finest hocks from Germany. But it might suggest, without presumption, that Canada has come farther along the route to good wine in its first 100 years than other countries did in theirs. Certainly the wines of South Africa and South America were slow starters; in both cases, a couple of centuries has to pass before there was any universal approbation. And, at an earlier stage in history, the improvement and growth of wines in European countries would have, of course, been far slower than the pace set in Canada.

Neither the grower nor the maker can take full

credit for this; the Canadian development has fortuitously occurred during the period of man's greatest strides in science, technical application and communication. Today the plant scientist in Kelowna can pick up the phone to check a fact with one in Guelph, a vine breeder in Ontario can exchange microscopic slides of parasites with another in California, the winemaker of Canada can share his knowledge with one in the U.S.S.R.

This isn't to discount the enthusiasm, the energy, the will, the pride, of those who in such a relatively short period of time have created good drinkable wines for the Canadian public. They have overcome huge problems, the rigors of the winter climate; an initial, paltry market; the ignorance and vindictiveness of the enemies of wine during the Prohibition period; the economic slump of the 1930's; the intervention of war; and much else. This is not to suggest they are demanding to be put on pedestals, and, indeed, it is too early to set up any Canadian Vintners' Hall of Fame. There is much to be done.

Three or four factors alone do not create the right smell, look and taste of wines; there are hundreds. Scores, even a hundred contributing factors, have been carefully analyzed but many more require careful scrutiny. It is not likely that there will ever be one wine so ideally supreme in Canada or anywhere else to please the taste of everyone, for there are more tastes (perhaps as many as there are fingerprints) than there are factors governing wine. The Canadian winemaker can never forget this, although in some provinces, he has daringly led public taste; the switch from high alcohol wines to table wines being the most notable example. Mainly, though, he has to be governed by public demand.

The Canadian seems well satisfied with the blended wines which are the native product, however, it is possible that in the future there may be some demand for vintage wine. It probably won't be immediate and, unless we become more affluent to an astonishing degree, more knowledgeable, and more selective, the demand won't be great. Some of the better winemakers are not uncognisant of this possible demand and do strive for a better wine each year; some hope that they will achieve a great wine.

But for the present, blended wines are to the liking of most people, as they provide a uniformly good quality product within the economic reach of practically all Canadians and are distinctively Canadian. They are not the same as California or New York State wines, and certainly not the same as European wines, and that is what Canadians who are drinking their own wines more than ever, like. They drink these wines in trains and planes, at home, at wine and cheese parties, in city hotels and restaurants. They also use them increasingly for wine cookery, which has not been mentioned before because it alone could form the subject of a complete book.

But there should be more places where Canadian wine is drunk. Nor should it have to be by the full bottle. How pleasant. for instance, would it be to break an afternoon's car journey in the countryside with a glass of amber-coloured table wine catching the sunlight in the garden of an inn. How relaxing, too, for the daily worker to halt for a moment at an urban cafe. How wondrous would it be to know that at the end of a long day's journey there would be, automatically, anywhere in Canada, some hotel or restaurant serving wine with dinner at a *reasonable* price.

All is within the realm of possibility. One has only to take a short glance over the shoulder at the receding years. Very, very recently in Canada wine was scorned. The derisiveness has now disappeared – very few now totally spurn Canadian wine.

It is true that we have no art, no music, no literature, no torrent of distinctively Canadian adjectives yet devoted to Canadian wine, but we do have enjoyment from it. Perhaps that is enough for some. But not quite enough for me, for that most difficult of words to define, ambience, is more essential to the proper appreciation of wine than any other food or drink. This does not mean it has to be rigidly imposed. It can come, unexpectedly, at noon-time in a sunny farmer's field among the corn stocks when the bottle is accompanied by fresh bread and cheese. It can be there with silverware and good conversation over a dinner table. It can be in a modest but magical restaurant setting.

Because of this, the winemaker alone, no matter how great his wines, cannot be the complete master. Appreciation of wines fully depends to a large extent on the temper of the times. The winemaker, the wine seller, must be like the playwright and his director – the wine's the thing – but so is the audience. No drama is great in an empty hall, nor can improved wines sell except to a selective public.

It won't be sufficient for the ten million gallonage or more of today to be doubled in the next ten years if that extra sale isn't of forever improving wines. Nor is it likely to take place unless the high standards of today are even higher. Canada, as a wine country, may have had a dynamic growth. In effect, its essential growth has been in the past quarter century. Before that, when poor wine was poured, the excuse could be made that the country was so concerned with basics, shelter and primary products, gaining solid foods and fuels, that there was no time for the niceties of life – and how many times have we all heard that reasoning to explain away the lack of novels or architecture or export trade during those early years. Now, however, there can be no excuses. We have more than 20 million people, which means Canada is a considerably bigger "market" than many nations have. We use the applied sciences as effectively and commonly as any people on earth. We are in the eyes of the world an efficient, trusted middle nation instead of a nonentity.

The wine industry fits into this evolving pattern. In 25 years it has become more than respectable. Its wines are now sought out, and if at least some who do so are driven by a degree of national fervor it can be a matter of pride that the product is such that they feel no shame in it.

These latter years then, as indicated more than once, have marked the transition of Canadian wines from a sometimes mewling, sometimes brawling, and sometimes sickly infant into adolescence. There has been a remarkable change. The industry, as good wine should, thrives. Some may say it is still too rambunctious, or, at the other extreme, too timid. It is the future years that will now count. It has been helped by the greater wealth, the greater cosmopolitanism, the greater education of Canadians in recent years. They, the audience, are going to have more to spend, travel other countries, and have more leisure in the future. All of these things will make them more critical, therefore it is likely that the public will want the best, or something close to it.

This may mean that some of today's less expensive wines may disappear and be replaced by better wines, as yet unnamed. On the other hand, with the possibility of even more Europeans settling in this land, the national consumption may soar so that the grape farmer and winemaker will be hard-pressed to serve the demand. Either way – and let's hope we get both – the men of Niagara and Okanagan face a considerable challenge. They must gauge the character and taste of their country as well as the clarity and body of their own wines.

May I suggest a toast to their success – in the Canadian wine of your choice.

Glossary

While the following is by no means a complete list of the words associated with wine, it is provided for those wine drinkers and wine lovers who wish to extend their knowledge of the terms associated with their favorite drink. Because wine is a universal beverage, terms are included which are common in Europe as well as those used in connection with Canadian wines.

ACID   The natural fruit acid contained in varying degrees in all grapes.

ACIDITY   The degree of tartness in a wine. All wines have some measure of tartness, indeed it is necessary not only in providing a good taste but good bouquet.

AGING   The process of allowing time to fully develop the character (essentially the good taste) of the wine.

APERITIF   This is sometimes called an appetizer wine. Usually served before meals and can be dry to semi-sweet. Sherry and vermouth are the most common.

AROMA   The fragrance of a wine that originates from the grapes. It is often fruity.

AROMATIC WINE   One with a strong fragrance, usually induced by blending certain herbs and spices with the wine.

ASTRINGENCY   A sharpness in wine which depends on the amount of tannin absorbed from skins, stems and seeds of the grapes.

BALANCE   The right proportion of sugar content and acidity in a wine.

BINNING   The task of storing bottled wines in bins for aging.

BLENDING   The highly specialized winemaker's craft of combining two or more wines to achieve a batch of wine of high standard and uniform quality.

BODY   The fullness or thickness of a wine. It cannot be measured except by the palate. Good wine can be of either heavy or light body.

BOTTLE FERMENTATION   A secondary fermentation which produces effervescence in the wine in the bottle.

BOTTLE SIZES A normal bottle contains about 26 fluid ounces; a magnum is two bottles, a jereboam can be equal to either four or six bottles, and a rehoboam can be equivalent to either six or eight bottles.

BOUQUET Fragrance of wine derived from fermentation.

BURGUNDY A dry red wine which can be either still or sparkling.

BRUT A French word indicating dryness in Champagne.

BUTT A Spanish sherry cask containing 108 gallons.

CANDLING An age-old method of examining the wine's clarity by holding the bottle to a candle.

CAPSULE A covering for the stoppers of wine bottles, usually made of metal foil or wax.

CARBON DIOXIDE A gas given off during fermentation of grapes.

CARAFE A container for serving wine in restaurants and hotels. They vary in size.

CAVES Underground cellars common in Europe.

CHARACTER A term used to describe the combination of taste, bouquet and colour of a wine.

CHAMPAGNE   A wine of high effervescence, white or pink. Originally made in the Champagne district of France.

CHATEAU BOTTLED   A term applied to French, notably Bordeaux, wines when the bottle label shows the chateau or vineyard where the grapes for the wine were grown.

CLARET   A dry red table wine.

CLEAN   A description for wine in which there are no tastes of yeasts or other additives used in winemaking.

CLOS   A word meaning enclosure and used to describe individual vineyards in France, particularly in Burgundy.

CLOUDY   A description for a wine containing suspended particles of grape skin, yeast cells or other matter.

CONCORD   The most common variety of grape in Canada.

CORK   The product of the cork trees of Portugal and Spain, still used in the bottling of many wines.

CORKY WINE   A wine with an unpleasant odor resulting from a diseased cork.

CRACKLING A description of mildly effervescent wines. They do not produce as many bubbles as sparkling wines.

CREAM A type of very rich sherry.

CRU A named vineyard.

CRUST The sediment of wine deposited in a bottle while aging. It is greatest in vintage ports.

CUVEE A special blend of wine, from which wines undergoing secondary fermentation in the bottle are frequently made.

DECANT To pour wine from one container to another.

DECANTER A glass bottle or carafe into which wine has been decanted for serving.

DELAWARE A grape variety grown abundantly in Canada.

DEMI SEC Half dry.

DEMIJOHN A container holding from three to eight gallons of wine.

DESSERT WINE A general description of usually medium-sweet to sweet wines with high alcoholic content (up to 20% by volume in Canada) .

DOSAGE   The sweetener added to sparkling wine after disgorging and before the final cork is put in the bottle.

DOUX   Sweet.

DRY   The opposite of sweet.

ESTERS   The compounds of alcohols and acids which give a wine its bouquet.

FERMENTATION   The process whereby sugars, by the action of yeasts, are broken down into alcohol and carbon dioxide. Through this process grape juice is changed into wine.

FILTERING   A method whereby wines are clarified.

FINING   The method of clarifying wine by additives which combine with sediment in the wine and carry them to the bottom of the wine vat.

FINO   The driest type of sherry.

FLAVOURED WINES   Grape wines that have had other fruit or herb flavours added.

FLOR   A yeast which gives sherry a distinctive taste.

FOCH   A variety of grape recently introduced into Canada.

FORTIFICATION   The process of adding brandy or grape spirit to dessert wines to increase their alcoholic content.

FOXY   A derogatory term for Canadian wine tastes.

HIMROD   A grape variety grown in British Columbia.

HOCK   An English term for any Rhine wine.

HOGSHEAD   A cask of varying size; in Bordeaux it contains 46 gallons, for Spanish sherry it is 52 gallons.

LEES   The sediment which settles on the bottom of a wine cask after the wine has been clarified.

MARC   The grape skins which are left after all the juice has been squeezed out by pressings.

MARRYING   The process whereby two or more different wines in a blend are allowed to remain in a tank or cask until the qualities of each is integrated with the other.

MATURITY   A state of wine achieved through aging.

MOUSY   A derogatory term for a wine having a musty ordor.

MUSCATEL   A dessert wine made from Muscat grapes and having a distinctively raisiny taste.

MUST Grape juice before and during the early stages of fermentation.

OXIDATION The change in wine caused by its contact with air.

NOSE A term signifying the bouquet of a wine.

PETILLANT Another word for crackling; slightly effervescent.

PINOT CHARDONNAY A high quality grape, now grown in Canada.

PINOT NOIR A high quality grape, also now growing in Canada.

PIPE A cask of varying measure. In Portugal it contains 115 gallons of port; in Madeira it contains 92 gallons of that island's wine; in France it is generally of 120 gallon capacity.

PORT A dessert wine, sweet and of high alcoholic content.

RACE A French term to denote breeding in a wine.

RACKING Drawing off a wine and putting it in another cask.

RIDDLING   The process of working the sediment down into the neck of the bottle during the secondary fermentation of effervescent wines.

RIESLING   A variety of grapes which produce well-known, distinctive white table wines.

ROSÉ   A pink-coloured table wine, which may be still or crackling.

SAUTERNES   A well-known variety of white table wine.

SEC   Dry as applied to the taste of wine.

SHERRY   A wine which may be used as an aperitif or dessert wine. It can range in colour from amber to dark brown, and has high alcoholic content.

SOLERA   A description of the blending method for sherry.

SPARKLING WINES   These are ones in which carbon dioxide is trapped during secondary fermentation to provide a bubbly effect when the bottle is opened.

SPLIT   A small bottle containing six- and-a-half to eight ounces of wine.

STILL WINE   A wine without effervescence.

TABLE WINE   A wine, which in Canada does not exceed 14% alcohol by volume, that can accompany food. It may be white, red or rosé.

TANNIN   An astringent acid found to some degree in all wines, but more so in red wines than white. The proper degree of tannic acid aids retention of high quality over long periods for fine wines.

ULLAGE   The loss of wine from a cask by evaporation or leakage.

VARIETAL WINE   A wine named for the principal grape variety from which it is made.

VERMOUTH   A dry or sweet aperitif wine flavored with herbs.

VINTAGE   The annual harvesting of grapes and making of the wine from them.

VINTAGE WINE   Wine made from a single year's production of grapes and labelled as such on the bottles.

VINTNER   A person engaged in winemaking.

WORMWOOD   A herb used in the preparation of vermouth.

YEAST   An organism whose fermentative qualities cause sugar to break down into alcohol.

References

Louis Pasteur: Pasteur Vallery-Radot; Alfred Knopf; 1958

Vintagewise: Andre L. Simon; Michael Joseph; 1945

The Commonsense Book of Wine: Leon Adams; David McKay, New York

Modern Wines: T. A. Layton; Heinemann; 1964

Encyclopedia of Wines and Spirits: Alexis Lichine; Random House; 1967

Encyclopedia Britannica: 1961 edition (for articles on wines, yeast etc.)

Encyclopedia Canadiana: The Canadiana Co. Ltd.; 1958 (articles on Canadian geography and climate etc.)

Wine Making for All: James Macgregor; Faber and Faber; 1966

Sherry: Rupert Croft-Cooke; Putnam; 1955

Quick Guide to Wine: Robert Jay Misch; Doubleday; 1966

The Technology of Wine Making: M. A. Amerine, H. W. Berg and W. V. Cruess; Avi Publishing Co., Westport, Conn; 1967

Notes on a cellarbook: George Saintsbury; Macmillan; 1923

An Alphabet of Choosing and Serving Wine: Raymond Postgate; Herbert Jenkins; 1955

Liquor: The Servant of Man: Morris Chafetz; Little, Brown and Co.; 1965

How Dry We Were: Prohibition Revisited: Henry Lee; Prentice Hall; 1963

The Penguin Book of Wines: Allan Sichel; Penguin Books; 1965

The Compleat Imbiber: edited by Cyril Ray; volumes one to eight; Holt Rinehart & Co.; 1957 et seq.

Treasury of Wine and Wine Cookery: Greyton Taylor; Harper & Row; 1963

The Wines of Australia: Harry Cox; Hodder and Stoughton; 1967

Sideboard and Cellar: A. B. Garrow; Musson Book Co.; 1950

Wine – Australia: Compiled by the Australian Wine Board; Nelson; 1968

In Praise of Wine and Certain Noble Spirits: Alec Waugh; William Sloane Associates.

The Fred Beck Wine Book: Hill and Wang; 1964

Folk Wines, Cordials and Brandies: M. A. Jagendorf; Viking Press; 1963

Grossman's Guide to Wines, Spirits and Beers: H. J. Grossman

A Wine Primer: Andre Simon

A Survey of Wine Growing in South Africa 1865-1966, the *Wine Grower in South Africa,* and several related booklets.